BETWEEN FRIENDS

By the same author:

A HEALING FELLOWSHIP
SET MY PEOPLE FREE
YESTERDAY'S CHILD
A CHILD NO MORE

BETWEEN FRIENDS

Overcoming the obstacles to friendship

Mary Pytches

HODDER AND STOUGHTON
LONDON SYDNEY AUCKLAND

British Library Cataloguing in Publication Data.

A catalogue record for this book is available from the British Library

ISBN 0-340-578319

Published by Hodder and Stoughton, a division of Hodder and Stoughton Ltd, Mill Road, Dunton Green, Sevenoaks, Kent TN13 2YA. Editorial Office: 47 Bedford Square, London WC1B 3DP.
Photoset by Phoenix Typesetting, Burley-in-Wharfedale, West Yorkshire.
Printed in Great Britain by Clays Ltd, St. Ives plc.

CONTENTS

INTRODUCTION

Many books have been written on the subject of marriage and family relationships. Not so many have been written about 'friendship': a close relationship which may exist between people of the same sex, the opposite sex or within a marriage.

When I think back over the years of listening to people's problems, it is the difficulties in relating and communicating which have featured most predominantly. In this book I explore some of the reasons behind these difficulties and give indications as to how we may overcome them and go on to enjoy rich friendships within secure boundaries.

In the beginning when God first made man, He said, 'It is not good for the man to be alone.'[1] As Billy Bray, the Cornish miner, used to say, 'Well, Father He do know best.'[2] And of course He does. Man is made to relate. Within the heart of every human being there is the longing to be known and to be loved. Yet many people, even in our Church Fellowships suffer intense loneliness in their search for someone with whom they may share their lives. This is not good. People who have few intimate relationships are ten times more prone to chronic illness and five times more likely to have a psychiatric disorder.[3]

Jesus said, 'Love the Lord your God with all your heart and with all your soul and with all your mind.' And then, 'Love your neighbour as yourself.'[4] When the principal relationship of a person's life is with God his basic needs for love and value are met. This knowledge of security and worth provides a strong base from which to relate to our fellow-man in a healthy, normal way. However, the fall created chaos, especially in human relationships – think how quickly Adam blamed Eve! We have moved

far away from God's original intention and it is hard to
find a way back. Therefore as we examine the blockages
and hindrances to a healthy friendship we must bear in
mind that each of these has its roots primarily in mankind's
separation from God. It is this estrangement from God
which still brings such pain into people's lives. So much
family life is troubled, and in many instances, damaging.
Children receive wrong teaching and poor modelling as
well as hurtful experiences which will later hinder them
from making normal relationships. But God, in His mercy,
has provided healing and restoration for any who will
turn to Him. He helps us in the removal of hindrances
and blockages and can heal the root causes, so that we
may go on to develop enriching friendships. Some time
and work may be called for but, as we shall see, the
benefits are well worth the effort.

Friendship is an exciting challenge. To help you make a
mature response to this challenge I have placed questions
for your consideration at crucial points in the chapters.
They are for the purpose of making you stop and think
about the way you relate to others and why you relate
as you do. The past could still be affecting your attitude to people in the present.

For those of you who are experiencing difficulty relating
closely to others because of unhealed hurt in your life I
have included a chapter outlining the process of healing.
After each step in that process I have included some tasks
which can mostly be done alone. I have also indicated
the times when it would be advisable to seek the help
of a mature Christian friend.

I owe a debt of gratitude to my husband David because
despite a very busy schedule he has made time, yet again,
to read and correct my manuscript. He is a true friend and
help meet. I am grateful also to the people who have shared
their relationship difficulties with me and given me food
for thought as well as material for this book. Lastly to my
friend and colleague, Prue Bedwell, I owe many thanks.
We became friends because God brought us together. We

have very dissimilar backgrounds and personalities and at
the time we met neither of us was particularly looking
for friendship. However, once we had become friends we
committed ourselves to be open and honest with each
other. Many times this has been painful and difficult but
it has paved the way for deeper understanding. The relationship has worked and many people have commented on
it, as the subsequent story illustrates. The secret, I believe,
has been having a common interest, a determination to
make it work and a mutual desire to do it God's way.

I have told the story elsewhere of the lady who came up
to me after Prue and I had spoken together at a conference.
She pointed at Prue and with tears in her eyes said, 'I want
one of those. I would like to have a friend like that.' I
remember thinking, 'Well, she could most likely have a
relationship like it if she was prepared to commit to the
work involved.'[5]

Friendships are not given us on a plate; they have to be
made, prayed about and worked at. I hope this book may
encourage people to make friends and keep them God's
way!

1

A DESCRIPTION OF FRIENDSHIP

Last year we visited the Carlsbad Caverns in New Mexico. When the idea was first suggested we asked a few preliminary questions. 'What exactly are they?' we enquired in our ignorance. 'How far away are they?' And, 'How long will it take to reach them?' The answers seemed satisfactory. So we seriously considered the prospect of descending the 830 feet into the bowels of the earth. First we had to decide whether we were fit enough. There was a three-mile trek into the cave by foot, before reaching the most impressive cathedral-like caverns with their incredible stalagmites and stalactites. Perhaps we should consider the short cut via a lift? Would special clothing be necessary? Were there any health conditions that could hinder a successful outcome to the expedition? This was the sort of normal preliminary research non-troglodytes like ourselves had to make before undertaking the exploration.

In exploring friendship the first question we must ask is the same one we asked with regard to the Carlsbad Caverns. 'What are we talking about?' Perhaps it would clarify matters if we first looked at what we are not talking about. Many relationships are called friendships which will not be the focus of our attention in this book.

Distant Friends
I know someone who has many friends. Some of them live abroad, and some in distant parts of this country. She corresponds or telephones these people regularly and always remembers their birthdays. Whenever she hears from them

or meets up with them she is delighted. Absence makes the heart grow fonder! Though these people certainly come into the category of friendship, nevertheless they place few demands upon her. Any annoying differences and irritating habits are too far removed to be bothersome. In these circumstances only the good seems to be remembered, and this of course in itself is delightful and refreshing, but the opportunity for such relationships to develop and grow through intimacy is essentially lacking. Distance prevents it. Precious as this sort of friendship is to many people it is not one we will be considering here.

Postal Friends

I have received many letters over the years from people wanting to develop a postal friendship with me. In books and from platforms I have often highlighted the vital part relationships play in one's growth. People then look around for someone to relate to. Frightened to move out of their comfort zones and meet the challenge of an eye-ball to eye-ball relationship they look for an easier option. A pen-pal! They may feel they know me or have identified strongly with something I may have said. But actually to relate to someone who lives many miles away, who knows very little about us and with whom we can be very selective in what we share, is not the sort of relationship which will provide the effective challenge most of us need.

I do not doubt there may be some enriching value in a postal friendship, especially as one grows older and travelling becomes tiring and making new friends more difficult. Letters between friends can be very comforting at such a time. Down through the ages friendship has been viewed as important. A hundred years before Christ was born Cicero said, 'Life is nothing without friendship.'[1] Therefore to keep in touch with friends in whatever way possible must enhance our lives.

Past Friends

We have friends from our time in South America with

whom we once shared our lives at a very deep level. Their friendship was at that time extremely important to us. These people are still our friends and several times a year we exchange news. But these can no longer be living, vibrant relationships. They exist more in our memories and our photo albums than in present reality. Were our situations to change they could hopefully be reinstated. But for now distance prevents the necessary access which makes the friendship viable.

Intermittent or Casual Friendship

Then there are people with whom one has immediate rapport and with whom one has much in common. Yet a meal and walk together now and then is all one can manage. Such people may be potentially ideal friends but lack of time and loyalty to other relationships prevent the friendship developing. Certainly proximity, time and priority are needed if a friendship is to become the vital, relevant and up-to-date relationship we will now consider.

Friendship

A relationship exists when there is a mutual sharing of life with another person, be it in play, work or the Church. A friendship exists when a relationship has the added dimensions of love, commitment and trust, as well as a high degree of mutual sharing. These four elements are foundational to any friendship, though other ingredients, which we shall mention in a later chapter, are needed to add richness and vitality.

In writing about friendship we are considering a relationship which could exist between a husband and wife, two women, two men or even two single people of the opposite sex. It would be true to say that, in their friendships, men differ somewhat from women. Their relationships are usually developed through a shared activity or a common interest. Men differ in their level of interaction and are more comfortable sharing opinions than feelings. Women's friendships appear to be more intense than men's, though

this may be because they are more able to show their
feelings to one another than most men. Even though these
differences do exist many men enjoy very rewarding and
rich friendships with one another. Strong feelings of loyalty
and compassion are to be found in their friendships, which
often last a lifetime. Probably the most famous friendship
of all time was between two men – David and Jonathan.

Within marriage friendship is not always the rule. Many
marriages are not based on friendship and, apart from the
family, the couple have few common interests. However,
when friendship does exist the foundational elements remain the same as they would in a relationship between two
people of the same sex. One could say that commitment
already exists because of the marriage agreement. However,
a commitment to work at the friendship is not necessarily
understood as part of the marriage agreement and it has to
be worked at in the same way as any other friendship.

So whether the friendship is between men or women,
married or single, the four elements mentioned are nevertheless necessary to the relationship.

Love

The psychiatrist, Dr Stack Sullivan, has said of love that
it exists when the satisfaction, security and development of
another person becomes as important as your own satisfaction, security and development.[2] There is a generosity
of heart about love. It sincerely desires material, emotional
and spiritual blessing for the one loved. 'Love is kind. It
does not envy.'[3] It is quick to encourage the other towards
growth and maturity. It is willing to sacrifice personal
comfort to meet the more urgent needs of a friend. St Paul's
famous description of love in 1 Corinthians 13 leaves one
gasping. One wonders how one can ever reach this 'most
excellent way'.[4] Yet without love, friendship cannot grow.

Sharing

We are talking about a relationship in which 'the continuing
debt to love one another'[5] applies equally to both parties.

Mutuality is another fundamental aspect of friendship. A one-sided friendship does not exist. Such a relationship would be better described as a counselling or helping one. In this case one person gives time and attention to another person but the roles are never reversed. In true friendship two people share their concerns and interests with one another.

There is an equality in friendship which usually does not exist in other relationships. Both give, both take, both love, both enjoy, both share. No one is exclusively in control. The one to whom it most pertains at that moment takes it up. For example, in the kitchen I normally take control, whilst maintaining the car is David's responsibility. This aspect of mutuality and equality makes it difficult for people in leadership to enjoy true friendship. Yet more than most they need the support and relaxation it provides. Commenting on the general failure amongst leaders to have personal friends, the writer and editor, Tom Marshall, suggests this may be the major contributing factor in leadership failure and burnout. Sensible principles for handling relationships of leaders, he feels, could be drawn up as apparently they were in the first Moravian community established by Count Zinzendorf in 1722. Their rules stated that the elders of the community were entitled to have their own friends and no one must take it amiss if others were more intimate with the elders than they were.[6]

I have talked with many clergymen and their wives who are dominated by an old-fashioned belief that neither the vicar nor his wife should have friends in the parish. Such couples are often lonely and isolated people whose lives are grey and impoverished. Not only do they lack enriching companionship but they also lack accountability which is such a healthy part of friendship.

Sharing of course involves some verbal communication. It is possible to have a close relationship with someone without a great deal of talking. A couple who have known each other for many years, either within marriage or in friendship, may not need to talk a lot. Being together is pleasure enough for both. However, even these exceptional couples need opportunity for real in-depth communication. Most people find that an important part of friendship is being able to share opinions freely, bounce ideas around, express feelings – both the good and the bad – and occasionally to share secrets.

Expectations of friendship vary greatly. Open discussion over the meaning of friendship is one way of avoiding disappointment later. However, most friendships develop gradually and such a discussion could inhibit a blossoming relationship. Only when difficulties occur is it necessary to air the differences. For example, one person may be rather organised and expect a friend to reserve time for a weekly appointment. The other person may not see the friendship in those terms, but rather in terms of availability at any time; preferring a much more easy-going friendship. At first the difference in expectation may not be noticed but gradually the dissimilarity will be felt and at that point open discussion is needed.

Trust

Charles Kingsley said that it was a blessed thing for any man or woman to have a friend – 'One human soul whom we can trust utterly, who knows the best and the worst of us and who loves us in spite of all our faults.'[7]

'The glory of friendship is not the outstretched hand,' said Ralph Waldo Emerson, 'nor the kindly smile, nor the joy of companionship; it is the spiritual inspiration that comes to one when he discovers that someone else believes in him and is willing to trust him.'[8]

Friends are trusted people who have access to one's person, one's family and home which others do not have. They share in one's troubles as well as joys and are even available in the middle of the night. The actress Marlene Dietrich said, 'It is the friends you can call up at 4 am that matter.'[9] Friends can be trusted with secrets. One can be vulnerable and weak with them. One can even be ill with them. For me this has been the most painful part of friendship. Yet inevitably it has opened the door to trust as nothing else has done. Sickness makes one defenceless and helpless. We do not have the same measure of control as when we are well.

My husband, David, was the only person I trusted enough to go on loving me even when he saw me at my worst. Many years ago I was forced to extend that trust. It was during our time in Chile. Our four girls were still small and we had suffered a very bad year of illness in which we had nearly lost one with peritonitis, another contracted tuberculosis, another had a serious kidney infection and I went down with hepatitis. At the end of that year I was worn out both physically and emotionally. One day my increasing anxiety overwhelmed me and I began to weep in desperation. Unbeknown to me a missionary friend was also in the house and heard my sobbing. Instead of shock and disgust she showed loving concern. Rather than shut me up, to my surprise she let me cry on her shoulder. Later we sat down together and talked through the problem of my growing anxiety. I agreed to every suggestion she made, including going to the doctor, because I trusted her. She had seen me at my worst and had not humiliated or rejected me. Though we have long been separated by oceans and continents my trust in her is as enduring as my gratitude.

Trust makes no contingency plans to protect oneself should the person trusted fail.[10] Trust puts one in a place of great vulnerability and the potential for hurt is then built into the relationship. This possibility of pain – which could be the outcome of trust – causes some people to forgo true friendship. Their failure to trust forces them to sacrifice the very intimacy which they long for.

Commitment

Finally for a relationship to become a friendship there has to be a commitment to it. A commitment is more than: 'I hope this friendship works,' or 'I would like it to grow.' Commitment actively keeps it working and growing. It does all that is necessary to foster a truly loving relationship. Commitment is a decision of the will. As John Powell says when talking about communication, 'It has to be a flint-hard posture of the will . . . no ifs and buts or time limits.'[11]

I recently heard someone state on the radio that 'love does not maintain a marriage. It is marriage that maintains love.' As I pondered the man's words I thought how wise he was. Love does not keep commitment alive. Commitment keeps love alive. Feelings of love are untrustworthy; they may come and go with the sunshine. It is commitment that makes love dependable not the feelings.

There are said to be three stages in love: optimism, disillusionment and commitment. During the optimism stage everything in the garden is rosy. We see no blemish in our new friend. He or she is everything we ever desired a friend to be. After a while, however, the rose-tinted spectacles come off and we begin to see the friend as he or she really is – as imperfect as ourselves! We then have the choice. To go our separate ways or to commit to the relationship. Commitment cements the relationship and makes a safe environment in which true friendship can develop in a mutually enriching way.

We have seen that the solid foundations on which a friendship rests are love, sharing, trust and commitment. The deeper and stronger the foundations the taller the building can be and the longer it will last. Walls, windows, doors and fittings will all be needed before it is complete. However, as soon as we can see the foundations we can form a good idea of the nature of the construction which can be developed.

To return to our visit to the Carlsbad Caverns. Once we knew what these caverns were and their distance from us, we asked the next question. 'What could prevent us making this journey and then descending into the depths of the earth?' Such things as lack of time, appropriate transport, illness or fatigue could have prevented us. The journey was obviously going to be a testing one and many times as we studied the maps someone would sigh and ask the question, 'Whose idea was this anyway?' The person whose idea it was would then extol the beauty and wonder of the caverns until once again we would all settle down to making our plans.

Despite the difficulties which surround friendship we should remind ourselves that the idea originated with God and the blessings make it worth the effort. 'Friendship improves happiness, and abates misery, by doubling our joy, and dividing our grief' (Joseph Addison, 1672–1719).[12]

2

WHOSE IDEA ANYWAY?

Margaret heaved a great sigh. 'Oh well, perhaps I'll get a cat instead,' she said. 'A cat instead of what?' I asked. 'A cat instead of a friend!' she replied.

Making and keeping friends may often be a difficult and complex operation and many of us can identify with Margaret's sigh of disillusionment. When we have inadvertently said the wrong thing, forgotten an important date or failed to read our friend's mind, we ask ourselves if it is really worth the hassle. Keeping a pet certainly seems easier. A pet's love is unconditional and they don't answer back. But although they do provide comfort and ease loneliness, they can never take the place of a genuine friend.

God's Idea
The idea of friendship originated with God. He exists in relationship and we are each made in the image of God. In the beginning He created the world in conjunction with the other members of the Godhead. The Son and the Holy Spirit both feature in the creation story. Although the doctrine of the Trinity is a mystery which our finite minds may never fully grasp, the story of creation gives one a glimpse of the unity of purpose that exists between the three persons of the Godhead.

When God created man He said, 'Let us make man in our image, in our likeness.'[1] By speaking in the plural He appears to emphasise the relational nature of the Trinity. Man is made in His image. Writing on this subject, Tom Marshall says that it is very important to understand that relationships form an essential part of man, made in the image of God. He agrees with Lawrence Crabb that relationships may be the essence of man's personhood as a God-imager, since relationships have existed within the Godhead from all eternity.[2]

God created Adam, placed him in the garden and then made an important 'maker's pronouncement': 'It is not good for the man to be alone.'[3] Man was not created to live in isolation; he was made for relationships.

In the first place we know that living in relationship was God's idea and that He was enjoying this Himself before He created people to do the same. In the second place we discover that God desires to have a relationship with us and even has friends amongst mankind. When the writer of the Proverbs wrote that there is a friend who sticks closer than a brother, he was surely alluding to the Lord.[4] God referred to Abraham as 'my friend'.[5] He spoke to Moses face to face 'as a man speaks with his friend'.[6] It was the manner in which these men communicated with God which singled them out as friends. God tells Miriam and Aaron, who spoke against Moses, that with other prophets He reveals Himself in visions, and speaks to them in dreams. But this is not true of His servant Moses; with him He speaks face to face, clearly, and not in riddles. Moses actually sees the form of God.[7] True friendship is identified by the intimacy, closeness and openness which exist between two people. They apparently speak 'face to face'. Also they communicate plainly and honestly. They do not have to use cover-ups, or innuendos.

Old Testament Friendships

Not only did close relationships originate with God but the Bible, God's word, puts a high value on friendship. 'So high indeed that most of what passes for friendship in our modern society is pallid in comparison.'[8] The most well-known and outstanding biblical friendships are between two men and two women; David and Jonathan, and Ruth and Naomi.

David and Jonathan first met after David had killed the Philistine giant, Goliath. It seems that they instantly recognised in each other a kindred spirit. 'After David had finished talking with Saul, Jonathan became one in spirit with David, and he loved him as himself . . . And Jonathan made a covenant with David because he loved him as himself. Jonathan took off the robe he was wearing and gave it to David, along with his tunic, and even his sword, his bow and his belt.'⁹ The friendship developed and Jonathan showed outstanding loyalty to David even in the face of his father's, King Saul's, animosity towards him. He was available to David, protective of him, felt able to make demands upon him and even saved his life. All of which are the marks of true friendship.

When they were eventually forced to part they made a commitment which went even beyond death. 'Then they kissed each other and wept together – but David wept the most. Jonathan said to David, "Go in peace, for we have sworn friendship with each other in the name of the Lord, saying, 'The Lord is witness between you and me, and between your descendants and my descendants for ever.'"' ¹⁰ When finally Saul and Jonathan are slain in battle David laments them both as great men and dearly loved, but he has a special lament for Jonathan. 'Jonathan lies slain on your heights. I grieve for you, Jonathan my brother; you were very dear to me. Your love for me was wonderful, more wonderful than that of women.'¹¹ David and Jonathan enjoyed a remarkable friendship which was valued highly by both of them. According to C. S. Lewis few modern people think friendship a love of value, or even a love at all. Yet to the ancients, friendship seemed the happiest and most fully human of loves. 'How has this come about?' he asks. 'The first and most obvious answer is that few value it because few experience it.'¹²

Two women who experienced a similar relationship were Ruth and Naomi. They became close friends despite their differences of age and background. Ruth's love for Naomi was strong enough for her to decide to leave her own people and country and go with Naomi back to Bethlehem. She made a firm commitment to Naomi saying, 'Don't urge me to leave you or to turn back from you. Where you go I will go, and where you stay I will stay. Your people will be my people and your God my God. Where you die I will die, and there I will be buried. May the Lord deal with me, be it ever so severely, if anything but death separates you and me.'[13] Their relationship also bore all the classic marks of a true friendship. They cared for one another, sacrificed for one another and were concerned for each other's well-being. Their friendship was a tremendous comfort to them and had a wonderful outcome. Ruth eventually married Boaz, a relation of Naomi's and the story ends with Naomi rejoicing in the birth of baby Obed who became the grandfather of King David, a forebear of Jesus Christ.

New Testament Friendships
We can learn much about friendship from Jesus. John felt himself to be especially close to Jesus and often referred to himself somewhat anonymously in the gospel as 'the one Jesus loved'. He was among the inner circle of disciples and at the Last Supper is seen sitting next to Jesus, even leaning back against his chest. He depicts Jesus living in close proximity to his disciples and at the same time enjoying a close relationship with his Heavenly Father. Jesus said that the love he had for his disciples sprang out of the love His Father had for him. 'As the Father has loved me, so have I loved you . . . Love each other as I have loved you. Greater love has no-one than this, that one lay down his life for his friends. You are my friends if you do what I command. I no longer call you servants, because a servant does not know his master's business. Instead I have called you friends, for everything that I learned from my Father I have made known to you.'[14]

When Jesus spoke these words he elevated friendship to the highest level. Friends should be prepared to make great sacrifices for one another. Friends communicate at a deep level. Friends spend time together and should be able to

depend upon one another for support and loyalty. Jesus
no doubt hoped to receive all this from his disciples but
when the moment of testing came they fell far short of
true friendship. He was left unsupported in the Garden
of Gethsemane. While he agonised over the prospect of
a cruel death his disciples simply slept. At his trial they
kept a safe distance. At his crucifixion only John and the
women stood near and watched. In his final moments Jesus
entrusted his mother to John. 'When Jesus saw his mother
there, and the disciple whom he loved standing near by, he
said to his mother, "Dear woman, here is your son."' And
John proved to be a trustworthy friend because, 'From that
time on, this disciple took her into his home.'[15]

The Acts of the Apostles and Paul's letters to the
churches, give some insight into the comfort and support
Paul received through his various relationships. Luke, the
physician, accompanied Paul on many of his journeys.
He was with Paul when he was tried by Felix and by
Festus. He sailed with Paul to Rome suffering the ship-
wreck with him. In the letter to the Colossians Paul
calls Luke, 'Our dear friend Luke, the doctor.'[16] Writing
to Timothy he says, 'Only Luke is with me.'[17] Other
men feature frequently in Paul's letters. There was Timothy whom he loved as a son and co-worker. There was
Tychicus, Epaphroditus and Onesimus, amongst others,
who are mentioned as being especially close to Paul. He
speaks of them with great affection.

King Solomon commends friendship when he states
quite simply and plainly, 'Two are better than one.'[18]
The examples of this chapter would seem to confirm
this. In the next we will examine the blessings which
come with a good friendship.

THE BLESSINGS OF FRIENDSHIP

'True friendship is like sound health, the value of it is seldom known until it be lost.'[1] The blessings which come with friendship often go unrecognised and unappreciated until the moment when one experiences the gnawing ache of loneliness which accompanies the loss of a friend.

My mother had several little maxims which she loved to recite at appropriate moments in the course of my childhood. 'Count your blessings,' was a favourite. Her idea of an appropriate moment was always when I felt least able to find anything for which to be happy or grateful. However, she was usually able to help me out and would think of several good reasons why I should be glad. Grudgingly I would then concede to one or maybe two blessings!

For the sake of those who need reminding that they should appreciate their friends more fully and for those who need encouragement to venture further along the road towards friendship, it is important to count the blessings of friendship. Man was not created to function well alone. Therefore when he does he is prone to exhibit some rather negative characteristics. In a healthy friendship these traits disappear.

Lost Traits
'An unfriendly man pursues selfish ends.'[2] Selfishness is inevitable for a person who lives without close friendship. Such a person has no pressing need to think of another's wishes. He needs only to consider his own. Loving another enough to desire that person's happiness and wholeness

prevents one from an unhealthy preoccupation with one-self. I have observed several transformations in people who before having a friend have been unable to see beyond their own problems. Their freedom from selfishness came through friendship.

My friend Margaret, who had jokingly suggested she get a cat instead of a friend (and maybe there was a hint of seriousness in the suggestion), was at that time struggling to sort out the difficulty of living with a close friend. She took time to think through all the pros and cons of sharing her life with her friend or of withdrawing altogether. Eventually she made her decision and rang to tell me what it was. 'I know that it wouldn't be good for me to live alone, nor do I want to,' she said. So she and her friend have worked out a way of sharing and at the same time providing each other with the needed space and freedom.

Introspection is another unhealthy trait which can haunt the lonely. Self-analysis is in vogue and the many DIY therapy books available make it an easy pastime. A friend helps one to focus outwards instead of inwards. Serious incidents, which would normally cause one to suffer agonies of self-doubt, have a way of becoming adventures when experienced with a friend. Just the other evening Prue Bedwell and I left a meeting at about 10.30 pm with more than an hour's travelling ahead. After about half-an-hour's driving we noticed that we were travelling north instead of south. If I had been alone I probably would have cried with frustration and then berated myself the whole journey. As it was we laughed and joked all the way home about the signs of senility we had been noticing in each other.

Depression is another problem which can be helped re-markably through friendship. I can hardly recollect ever meeting a depressed person who was also involved in a close and vibrant friendship. Somehow the two things do not go together. Depression has many causes, therefore it would be wrong to generalise. However, when a person is suffering from a reactive depression the cause is often a loss of some sort. The loss of a spouse, job, pet, or parent may happen to any one of us and loss is always painful. When borne alone with no one to talk to and no shoulder to cry on the result may be depression. As we said in the introduction those who have few intimate relationships are ten times more prone to chronic illness and five times more likely to have a psychiatric disorder.

The blessing of friendship does not stop with the negative things we lose. Friendship adds to one's life in many positive and beneficial ways. In fact to compile an exhaustive list would be impossible. Nevertheless some of the advantages are especially worth a mention.

Challenge

Alone it is easy to settle down into a rut and never be challenged to move beyond one's limitations. When I first met David there were many things I had made up my mind I would never do. I would not eat onions, curry, or Chinese food. I would not drive a car nor sew. I was afraid of hospitals and flying. David challenged my limitations and protesting loudly I started to move out of my self-imposed restrictions towards a more exciting life style.

Friends challenge our too-cosy way of life. They also challenge the way we are as people. 'We need others physically, emotionally, intellectually; we need them if we are to know anything, even ourselves.'[3] I cannot know myself in isolation. My friends hold up a kind of mirror for me to see myself. Without this mirror I could remain ignorant of an unattractive trait, an irritating habit or an unhealthy attitude. A trusted friend can challenge these unacceptable mannerisms. 'Faithful are the wounds of a friend.'[4] Faithful because 'Love never wounds unless the wound is for the greater good of the person wounded.'[5] It can be uncomfortable, even painful to see oneself through the eyes of another person. Nevertheless if friendship is to be beneficial it has to contain mutual loving confrontation which is a significant part of all good human relationships. Without it the relationship is unfruitful and shallow.[6]

Charlie and Dave's friendship had developed to a point where each could speak the truth without risk of losing the relationship. 'He doesn't let me get away with anything,' Dave said to me, describing the way Charlie helped him. The trust which now existed between the two men provided a perfect environment for mutual and beneficial challenge.

In the process of growing up we form assumptions about life. These assumptions develop from the teaching and modelling of our parents and from past experience, both good and bad. Those which have been formed as a result of past experience always seem to our minds to be especially logical and reasonable. We rarely challenge these basic assumptions and need others to do this for us. My family was a non-church-going family and as I grew up I presumed that God was unimportant to life, that is if He existed at all. When I left school I lived in a hostel with other young people and we enjoyed many debates about life in general. On one occasion someone started a discussion about faith. I remember several young girls challenging my agnostic stance. I defended myself energetically but inside I was greatly disturbed by their convictions over the existence of God and from that moment on I began to seek Him.

Basic assumptions which are formed out of teaching and experience are the most difficult to shake off. When I lived in South America I had a friend who was rather wealthy and aristocratic. She had been brought up to think the poor were of less value than her kind of people. Her experience of some dishonest and lazy characters compounded this misconception. We became friends when she became a Christian. One evening we went together to hear a visiting preacher. He spoke on 'loving one's neighbour'. At the end we were asked to get up and do the sort of thing that makes the average Englishman curl up. He told us to hug our neighbour, but not the person we had come to the meeting with. I was sitting on one side of my friend and on her other there was a gap. At the far end of the row was an elderly, rather grubby-looking woman. She looked

like a tramp who had come in off the street for warmth
and somewhere to sit. My Chilean friend hesitated and
then went up and gave the old woman a hug. All the
way home she was silent. Sitting elegantly in my sitting
room later she looked miserably at me and said, 'I did
it, but I didn't.' 'What do you mean?' I asked her. She
explained how she had looked at the old woman and
had been repulsed, but then she felt she couldn't refuse
to do as she had been asked if she really professed to be a
Christian. So she went through the motions, but inwardly
she had still rejected the poor old soul. We talked for a
long time that evening, and many more times after that.
Gradually the beliefs she had held all her life began to
change. Today there are many poor people living in that
part of Chile who have had reason to bless my friend for
her love and generosity since that time.

A healthy friendship challenges one to change and grow.
'As iron sharpens iron, so one man sharpens another.'[7] In
our western world hundreds of people are prepared to pay
another human being simply to listen to their problems
and help them find a resolution. Friendship will often
serve this function almost unintentionally. 'Perfume and
incense bring joy to the heart, and the pleasantness of one's
friend springs from his earnest counsel.'[8] In a counselling
relationship one person listens to another's problems, asks
questions to clarify issues, helps the counsellee to see the
problem from different points of view, may make a few
suggestions and then prays with the counsellee. Unless
there is an unhealthy emotional enmeshment, friendship
should be able to provide all this. When people first come
for counselling with me I nearly always ask whether or not
they have a close friend, not excluding a spouse, with whom
they feel totally safe. Most of them say they have friends
but on further questioning they rarely have a close friend
whom they would trust with their problems and who would
be prepared to listen and if necessary to challenge them.
So they have no opportunity, other than counselling, for
working through their difficulties in a safe setting.

Friendship is a profound comfort but a monumental challenge.[9] Most of us are attracted more by the comfort than the challenge. But the growth and change that can occur through real friendship are wonderful benefits, and the comfort is there to offset the challenge.

Comfort

'If one falls down, his friend can help him up. But pity the man who falls and has no-one to help him up! Also, if two lie down together they will keep warm. But how can one keep warm alone? Though one may be overpowered, two can defend themselves.'[10] This is a quote from King Solomon who depicts a friend as a helper, a comforter, and a strength. Each one a blessing well worth counting.

A while ago, during a time of particular stress, friends rang us and said that they thought David and I were looking rather jaded and they wanted to take us out for the day. We had a complete change of scenery looking over a glorified antique junk yard near Guildford and then on to a local pub for lunch. Our friends' kind and imaginative invitation, which they knew we would enjoy, gave us just the break we needed.

Whenever we minister away from our home base it is wise to follow the model Jesus set with his disciples when he sent them out in twos. In isolation we are open to a whole range of negative thoughts and temptations. With a friend it is easier to avoid these traps of the enemy. On a recent ministry trip to Germany our aeroplane skidded off the runway as it was taking off and came to a shuddering halt. I have never liked flying and this just seemed to prove how stupid I was to trust myself to such a dangerous method of transport! Fortunately I was with a friend who calmly talked me through to common sense and composure. There was no other way after all to reach our destination on time.

'The loneliness of a world that has a population of one is filled by a new and warm presence when love enters a life.'[11] The love of a friend is a comforting experience. It is also a joyful one.

Joy

When John the Baptist was describing the joy he felt at
the coming of Jesus, he compared it to the joy that the
bridegroom's friend feels at the sound of the bridegroom's
voice.[12] The sound of a friend's voice always brings joy. For
this reason the telephone is such a blessing. When David
and I were engaged to be married and living in different
parts of the country we used to write to one another every
day, but the highlight of the week was the telephone call
on Saturday evening. We could say so little and the time
was so short, but the sound of the voice was enough.

To be alone and friendless is such an empty existence.
The writer of Ecclesiastes calls it a 'meaningless, miserable
business'. And he points out that 'two are better than one
because they have good return for their work'.[13] Working
together is not only more fun and more satisfying but it
also brings in a better harvest. Washing-up, gardening,
house decorating, addressing envelopes; such work when
done alone can be slow and boring, but when done in the
company of a friend can not only be achieved more quickly
but can also be fun.

Magnificent scenery or a beautiful sunset can be even
more fully appreciated when shared with another. After
his wife was killed, the writer Tom Marshall said that
he was aware that whenever he was given a profound
insight, or had a deep experience, he had a sad sense
of something that would be lost or of something which
would die with him because there was no one to share it
with.[14] Peak experiences are enhanced when shared with
a friend and joys shared have a way of enriching the
relationship.

St John wrote to the 'chosen lady and her children', that
he really wanted to visit her rather than write a letter.
'I hope to visit you and talk with you face to face, so
that our joy may be complete.'[15] The sight of a friend's
face gives joy. It may be an old, lined face or a young,
smooth face. It really doesn't matter. By the time the
rough crossing from being a new friend to becoming an old

friend is made, looks are no longer a priority. Comfortable familiarity is of far greater value than a handsome face. The reappearance of a friend after an absence, however long, is a joyful experience. David came back from a London meeting recently overjoyed because he had met an old friend he had not seen for over forty years.

The great blessing of Christian friendship is the knowledge that there is always help close at hand. Also that, although there may be times of absence, there will never be a real separation.

Security

'A cord of three strands is not quickly broken.'[16] The secret of a permanent friendship is found in the presence of a third strand. Without God's presence the relationship may be, for a while, a challenging, comforting, joyful experience, but life is not easy and no relationship can ever be problem-free. Only when a couple seek to live under God's rule and together pray, 'Thy will be done on earth (and in our friendship) as it is in Heaven,' will those problems begin to turn into blessings and become a means of growth for them both.

Any friendship can fail, but a Christian one should be less likely to. The Holy Spirit has been sent to be our teacher and helper, and He has a way of giving us a nudge when our words or actions have been unloving. If we have been hurt He quickly reminds us to forgive because as we forgive so we are forgiven. To be able to talk about one's differences and then to pray together is an amazing bonus in a Christian relationship.

Sadly friendships come to a temporary end. This may sometimes be through having to move, as we had to from South America, but it may be through death. Whatever the cause, part of the great Christian hope is that one day we will be reunited with our friends in Glory. There God will wipe every tear from our eyes. There will be no more death or mourning or crying or pain, for the old order of things will have passed away.[17]

Meanwhile as we travel together with our friends on the journey of life enjoying the shared experiences let us count the blessings as we go. Helen Keller was blind, deaf and dumb and humanly speaking had little to be happy about. Yet due to her many friends she enjoyed a rich and varied life. She said, '. . . It is that my friends have made the story of my life. In a thousand ways they have turned my limitations into beautiful privileges, and enabled me to walk serene and happy in the shadow cast by my deprivation.'[18]

There is no doubt that a loving friendship leads to a fuller life. 'It is only in the experience of love that a human being can know himself, can love what he is and will become, and find the fullness of life that is the glory of God.'[19]

Prayer
Heavenly Father I give you thanks for every friend I have ever had. Each one has brought something special into my life. I thank you for . . . and . . . and . . . *(name of friend and the special quality which he or she brought into your life)*. Father I want to thank you for the friendship I am enjoying with . . . at this moment. I thank you for him *(or her)* and for the challenge *(name the way in which he or she has challenged you)*, the comfort *(name the special comfort he or she has brought into your life)*, and the joy *(mention some of the joyful experiences you have shared together)* I have experienced. I thank you that whatever happens we will always be friends and that in your Kingdom there is no ending to love. Amen.

As we have already suggested for some people friendship is not all plain sailing. For most the rewards of friendship are enough to encourage them to either work through, or patiently tolerate the problems. However, there are others for whom the problems seem insurmountable. In the following chapters we will look more closely at some of the negative characteristics which could hinder people from making or keeping friends.

4

HINDRANCES TO MAKING FRIENDS

'How good and pleasant it is when brothers live together in unity. It is like precious oil poured on the head . . . It is as if the dew of Hermon were falling on Mount Zion. For there the Lord bestows his blessing.'[1]

We may believe this psalm to be true and long to enjoy the benefits of such friendship and yet find ourselves regularly foiled in our attempts to make close friends. The reason for this may be that we are unconsciously holding some false assumptions about relationships. It is these which hinder us from possessing the very thing we long for. Although recognising these misconceptions will not of itself correct them, nevertheless acknowledging that we have a problem and understanding why we have one, are the first steps in making the necessary changes. Therefore it is worth spending some time considering the following misconceptions and asking ourselves whether one of these could be causing the blockage.

Home is where we make our earliest and most formative assumptions about relationships. One's family of origin does not have to be totally bad for it to be dysfunctional. Particularly in the area of personal relationships parents can fail to give a good model. Children from such homes will know about the unhealthy ways of relating but very little about the good. They will grow up with distorted ideas of what is normal. They will have formulated some ideas about relating which to their minds will be perfectly appropriate but in fact reflect the poor modelling and bad experiences of their childhood. Such beliefs could mar all future attempts at making healthy friendships.

A dysfunctional family is inept at communication and rarely brings into the open issues that are causing undercurrents of anxiety, jealousy or resentment. Parents in such families are usually so preoccupied with business or personal problems that they are unable to be emotionally present for a child, and the normal loving is constantly being interrupted. In such cases the family system is one in which a child may form beliefs that could be a hindrance to him in the future. At the same time he may also have stored up some very painful feelings which unfortunately do not dissipate with time. These have a tendency to stay buried within the child only to re-surface in the future at the slightest provocation.

Such **thoughts** and **feelings** become the driving power behind **behaviour**. Take the case of a woman who was quite unable to relate to anyone of the opposite sex. She had in fact been sexually molested by her father during several years of her childhood. Although she had successfully suppressed the memory of the experience she had retained a belief that men were not to be trusted. She also felt very frightened in their presence, especially if she was left alone. These thoughts and feelings caused her to take avoidance action. She would plan never to be alone with any man. She would endeavour never to sit within close proximity to a male. If she ever found herself accidentally doing so she would find a way to make a quick exit. Her thoughts and feelings, not the memory of the experience, were the driving force behind her behaviour.

In most cases of people who are consistently unable to make close relationships it is worth noticing that the primary emotional response is anxiety or fear. Other feelings may be lurking about, but fear is the dominant emotion.

Fear is a normal human response to danger and serves to protect one from harm. A person without the normal 'flight and fight' response has a potential problem with

survival. Fear can therefore be seen as a healthy protection.
It can also be a reaction to an immature interpretation of
a past experience. Let us remember that, 'children are very
good recorders but poor interpreters'. A child may have
accurately recorded an incident of rejection but then she
incorrectly tells herself that this must mean she is a bad
person. The fear of anyone discovering this awful truth is
then trapped within the child. However, it can be stimulated
involuntarily any time someone tries to come too close.

If you identify with one of the following beliefs the questions listed for consideration at the end of each misconception may help you think more deeply about the problem.

1. *Misconception* – **'If people really knew me they would
    not like me.'**
    Emotion – **Fear, anxiety, guilt, shame.**
    Behaviour – **Hiding, wearing a mask, distancing from
    people.**

A child who has heard a parent or authority figure criti-
cise her over and over again with such phrases as, 'You are
stupid. You never get anything right,' may eventually come
to believe this to be true. Or perhaps a parent or teacher
used a lot of shaming as a means of disciplining: 'You disgusting child. You should be ashamed of yourself.' Hurtful
words for a child, but when shouted in front of others they
shame a child and deeply mar his own self-image.

I remember when I was about eleven years old being
falsely accused of lying to a teacher at my boarding school.
I tried to explain that there must have been some mistake
but to no avail. I was punished and sent to bed early.
The punishment fitted the perceived offence, and though it
smarted to be wrongfully accused, I would have recovered
my normal buoyancy in a few days. However, the teacher
was unable to leave it at that. Our school had a guide
company which I had just joined. The next Friday evening
I proudly donned my new uniform and turned up for the
meeting, only to be told that I had been suspended because,
'guides do not lie'. I felt very upset, but worse was still to

come. During the preliminary part of the evening when the whole company met together for opening prayers, I was called out to the front to hand over my badge to the captain. I was mortified and shamed. Needless to say I never went to another guide meeting, and six months later when I was told that they would now have me back, I enjoyed telling them that I had other interests!

Fortunately this sort of shaming was not a frequent occurrence in my own experience but for a child for whom it is, thoughts gradually form and a particular fear takes root: 'Something about me must be bad, disgusting, horrible, unlovable. Anyone who comes too close will reject me. I must take great care to hide this part of myself away.' The child has been fed a lie and believes it. The adult may later know rationally that this is not really true but at gut level the lie remains and determines the victim's behaviour.

The fear of criticism and rejection causes a person to hide behind a mask. On the outside he puts on the 'nice' person, a person who seeks to please; a person who seldom gives a personal opinion. He will rarely show sadness or anger. All the aspects of his personality he considers 'bad' he will keep hidden behind the mask. He has in fact developed a 'pseudo-self'. This makes him anxious when people around him start asking personal questions. 'Choosing to fake it means that one must learn to cope with the free-floating anxiety that comes from living a lie.'[2] He lives with a sense of guilt and shame and at the end of the day is very lonely because he has allowed no one in close enough to be a true friend.

For Consideration:
Did you receive a lot of criticism or shaming as a child?
Do you wear a mask?
Do you feel anxious when the conversation becomes personal?

2. *Misconception* – **'If anyone comes too close I will be trapped.'**
   Emotion – **Fear, revulsion, anger.**

Behaviour – **Avoidance of controlling types, and of confrontation, possible homosexual tendencies.**

Incest is one of the causes of the love process being interrupted. Physical incest has horrific consequences in a person's life and it may take many years for the wounds to heal. Many carry them to their graves. Emotional incest can also have a profound effect upon a child. This occurs when a parent is not getting his needs for intimacy met at the adult level. It could be through illness of a partner, absence, or incompatibility. In several cases of people I have counselled the problem has been one parent's alcohol abuse which has left the other parent isolated. The lonely parent then seeks to meet his or her intimacy needs with the child. This never fails to have a detrimental effect. The child may at first enjoy the closeness and attention, but in time feels trapped by the demands of the one who is close. Future relationships could then be hindered by a fear of being possessed and controlled once again.

This fear is often present in the homosexual. As we have already seen sexual abuse may cause a woman to fear men. She may then attempt to meet her intimacy needs with other women. Conversely a man who has been engulfed by a demanding mother could feel repulsed by women and flee their presence. He may feel that only men are safe to love. As former homosexual, Andy Comiskey, writes: 'The dominant mother . . . breeds fear of women, gender confusion, perfectionism, contempt. The young man detaches from her, a breach that generalises on to all women. She is internalised as untrustworthy and false – the move away from her is a developmental rupture, not one of healthy separation into adulthood. The result is an unnatural reliance and idealisation of man.'[3]

One young man who had been swamped by a controlling, lonely mother was paralysed by fear every time a girl made overtures of friendship. He felt trapped by her nearness and threatened by her needs. Yet he seemed unable to extricate himself from the relationship in the normal way.

His solution was usually to move away or to disappear without trace.

In some cases an adult is hindered from making friends because the controlling parent is still making demands. Separation from parents and a growing independence is the major task of childhood. This task is normally facilitated by encouragement and help of parents. But in the case of a needy or overly controlling parent this may not happen. Instead of a normal, healthy bonding with parents which enhances growth there is an unhealthy, emotional bondage which snuffs out the normal attempt of the child to become an autonomous individual. In many cases the parent has no desire to hurt the child, in fact he or she would insist that he loves his son or daughter very much and only wants the best for him or her. At the same time the parent makes unnatural emotional demands upon his offspring. This demand may continue past the age when the child should clearly have become independent.

Alice went into counselling because of a long-term problem with depression and ill-health. She was forty-five and still living at home. Both her parents seemed upright people but they lived their lives through their only daughter. They had cared for her, sacrificed for her and doted over her. However, she herself had no friends and seemed to lack the capacity for making them. It took many years of counselling to set her free from the emotional bondage to her parents and enable her to take steps towards independence. Friendship with one or two safe people has slowly developed since.

For Consideration:
Do close relationships cause you to feel trapped?
What was your relationship like with your parent of the opposite sex?
Do you still feel in any way emotionally bound to one or both of your parents?

3. *Misconception* – 'Loving inevitably means losing.'

Emotion – **Fear, sadness, loneliness, abandonment, sometimes depression.**
Behaviour – **Chooses isolation.**

Listening to a talk on courage I was interested to hear the speaker say that it takes courage to love. The possibility of pain is always present if one truly loves. He described the day his oldest daughter was born and he caught his first glimpse of her; a tiny premature baby in an incubator. He said that as he looked at her he fell totally in love with her. He realised that for the rest of his life he would be profoundly affected by whatever should happen to her.

The danger of loss always accompanies love but normally this will not prevent a person from making a loving relationship. But if a person has already lost someone to whom they were deeply attached or at some stage in his childhood lived under the threat of losing someone important to him through parental conflict or illness, then loving will inevitably seem to pose a real threat of loss. At the same time such a person may be carrying some unresolved feelings with regard to the experience of loss. The suppression of bad feelings is a far more normal occurrence in our western society than is the healthy expression of them.

During a conference we were conducting on healing, an elderly man of about seventy-five asked for prayer for a recurring headache. A married couple agreed to pray with him. He was encouraged to open himself up to the work of the Holy Spirit and as he did so he began to cry. At first he cried quietly but then the crying increased until he was sobbing like a small, abandoned child. The memory which the Holy Spirit had surfaced came from the time when he was five years old. He had been woken in the night by his older brother coming into his room and getting into his bed with the comment, 'Mother has just died.' At this point his father had come into the room and addressed the brother. 'Have you told him?' he asked. 'Yes,' said the brother. That was the last time he could remember his mother ever being mentioned in his family. The five-year-old boy was never given an opportunity to ask his questions about where she had gone, or what had happened to her, nor to express his terrible grief at losing the most precious and important relationship of his short life. For seventy years he had suppressed the feelings connected with that grief. Certainly the recurring tension headaches were one of the consequences of that suppression. No doubt he suffered other effects which he had never linked to that traumatic event when he was five years old.

Sadly a person dominated by a fear of loss usually chooses aloneness when in fact it is the one thing they most dread. Feelings of abandonment may haunt them and yet the fear keeps them trapped in lonely isolation.

For Consideration:
Can you remember being in danger of, or actually losing, someone you loved when you were younger?
Do you choose to be alone when in fact you would prefer to be with others?

4. *Misconception* – **'Don't trust anyone. People are never there when you need them.'**
   Emotion – **Fear, mistrust, anger.**
   Behaviour – **Independence, denial of normal needs, overly self-controlled.**

The well-known psychiatrist, Erik Erikson, suggests that trust vs. mistrust is the major issue in the first months of every baby's life.[4] My prayer for every new addition to the growing ranks of our own grandchildren is that the parents and baby will thoroughly enjoy and delight in one another during those early weeks. I long for the babies to receive all the right signals about themselves and the world around. They need to know that they are valued and loved, that their parents are trustworthy and that their relationship is something mutually precious.

When a new-born and his mother joyfully bond, trust is built into the foundations of the personality. Such good impressions will be impossible to eradicate later. On the other hand a baby or toddler who has been consistently

left to cry with discomfort by unreliable, thoughtless or
misguided parents, will make mistrust the starting point for
every future relationship. Inconsistency and unreliability
will, in their minds, be an inevitable part of relating.

In one sense it is true that people are not always available
when needed and providing there are no unresolved bad
feelings this is acceptable to most of us. However, a person
who carries around within him the buried memories of
needing someone and no one being there for him, will make
every effort to avoid a similar situation in the future. This
person may make friends but he does not fully trust them
to come too close. He believes he must avoid being in the
position of needing them and then being let down when they
are not there for him. It is amazing how such a person will
often prove early on in a relationship how untrustworthy
the new friend is by needing him just at the moment the
friend is not available. After this he feels perfectly justified
in keeping the friend at arm's length. He may continue with
the relationship but only at a safe distance.

A young man came into counselling with a problem he
was experiencing in a current relationship. His girlfriend
seemed very keen to have the relationship go further, but
he was hesitant. As this same reluctance had been the cause
of other girlfriends leaving him he had decided to seek some
help. After just a few weeks of counselling the cause of his
reluctance became obvious. The counsellor had to go away
for a few weeks and when this was explained to the young
man he became very angry. 'I knew I should never have
trusted you. You go away just when I need you.' As the
angry feelings were examined a host of childhood memories
were stimulated. Both mother and father had been very
busy and were never around at the most important moments
of this young man's life. He had buried his anger and disappointment and enabled himself to manage without them.
But a hardness developed in his heart towards any who tried
to come too close. The hardness was partly there as a protection against further disappointment but also it was a way
of punishing those he had already judged as unreliable.

For Consideration:

Were your parents usually available to you when you needed them?

Do you feel just disappointed or very angry when you are let down?

Which do you prefer to be? Independent, dependent or inter-dependent.

5. *Misconception* – 'I hurt people.'
   Emotion – Fear, self-hatred.
   Behaviour – Solitary activities. Unfriendliness.

If a child is told often enough that she is to blame for the sickness of her mother, the trouble in the family or the hardwork and exhaustion of her parents, she will eventually conclude that she must be bad for people because she makes them sick, troubled or exhausted. Instead of achieving a sense of worth, feelings of self-hatred take root.

Angie is such a person. She was consistently blamed for her mother's unhappiness and pain. Inevitably she grew up with the belief that she hurt people who came too near to her. She became a lonely recluse, always siding with the under-dog. Although several people tried to come alongside her she would just repeat her now customary spiel. 'I can't get too close because I will only hurt you.' Her mother had long since died but Angie kept her accusations alive within her. These false allegations imprisoned Angie as severely as a convict behind bars. Not only was she trapped by her repetition of a totally absurd belief but also by her fear of dropping the only identity she had ever known. Her whole attitude to life seemed inextricably entwined with this false assumption, 'I hurt people.'

A person with a low self-image will often choose aloneness because he is afraid of seeing what he fears about himself reflected in another person's eyes. His excuse for opting out of the relationship may be that he is no good at friendship and hurts people. Yet another may choose to be alone because it is easier that way. Relating to others can be difficult. More than anything else friendship smooths our rough edges and changes us. But change is uncomfortable and rather than push through the pain barrier the same excuse may be used.

For Consideration:
Were your parents proud of you?
How would you describe yourself? Use three positive adjectives before using any negative ones.
Could these attributes be a blessing to a friend?

6. *Misconception* – 'I don't need other people.'
   Emotion – Anger, scorn, free-floating anxiety at times.
   Behaviour – Independence from others. Needs to be in a position of control. Adopts a stance of superiority.

Rick was a mystery to everyone. People were attracted to him and would like to have known him better but they were afraid to make too many overtures for fear of being rebuffed. He usually turned down invitations to meals though sometimes he would agree and then not turn up. He gave himself sacrificially to helping anyone in trouble. Yet he never seemed to get close to anyone. He actually believed that it was a sign of weakness to need other people. He scorned any kind of weakness or vulnerability within himself and gave the appearance of strength and control.

In fact, Rick had a terror of becoming dependent upon another person in any way. In his efforts not to lean towards another human being he leant in the opposite direction – away from human relatedness.

Writing about this 'need love' C. S. Lewis said that not to feel it was generally the mark of a cold egoist. He writes, 'The illusory feeling that it is good for us to be alone is a bad spiritual symptom; just as lack of appetite is a bad medical symptom because men do really need food.'[5]

This total rejection of normal needs is sometimes due to great pain. The psychiatrist and author, Frank Lake, described it as a position that an infant has been driven to by the failure of human persons to provide sustained personal relationships. He suggests that this failure may give rise to great mental pain and once the margin of tolerance is passed a paradoxical state is entered in which all desire for life through personal relationships has been extinguished. The infant simply does not want to live by investment in relationships.[6] Dr Lake is describing a person with a commitment anxiety who cannot bring himself to enter a mutually caring relationship. Though he may concede commitment in caring for others, he will not do so for himself.

This would describe Rick's position. His fear of commitment was overwhelming and he was very hard on himself; not allowing any vulnerability or weakness to surface. Yet he would care for others who were needing his help. By repeating his belief that he did not need anyone and by getting angry with anyone who tried to come close he kept himself safe from danger – the great danger of falling over the edge into despair if he ever needed someone who failed to come.

For Consideration:
Were you a very independent child?
Do you get anxious if people come close to you?
Do you find it easy to care for others?
Can you allow others to care for you?

Dysfunctional families cause distorted perceptions and painful emotions which take root within a child but later produce bitter fruit. This fruit most frequently shows up in relationships. As we have seen, a person may be hindered from even attempting to relate closely. On the other hand he may enter into friendship only to spoil it by his irrational thinking, bad feelings and unhealthy behaviour patterns. We shall now examine some of the obstacles to maintaining a healthy friendship.

5

OBSTACLES TO MAINTAINING
A HEALTHY FRIENDSHIP

Hilary and her husband were experiencing problems in their
marriage. She had been feeling increasingly depressed and
had lost any desire for physical intimacy. This had caused
him to feel cheated and so he had retreated into an angry
silence. She was also beginning to withdraw from other
close friends.

Although we may be aware that our thinking affects our
behaviour, we often remain ignorant of what that thinking
is and where it comes from. Hilary seemed quite oblivious
to what had caused her problems. Only as she allowed her
feelings to spill over did the truth emerge. In the safety
of the counselling room she began to express feelings of
anger and resentment towards her husband because she
felt second-best in his life. In fact she felt left out in the
cold by him and by other close members of the family
as well. When questioned she admitted that these feelings
were not new to her. In her childhood she had felt this
way most of the time. Her parents had only two children
and the oldest was a boy upon whom they doted. His
father was very proud of him and his mother made a
great fuss of him. She had always felt second-best and
little valued. Now her husband was giving a lot of time
to his job; other members of the family were occupied with
work and friends and she was feeling increasingly isolated.
The situation revived old assumptions about herself and
activated her feelings of anger, resentment and depression.

This was followed by a strong desire to withdraw herself.

Once we recognise the thinking and feelings behind our behaviour we are part-way towards resolving our problems.

It is possible to pin-point several misconceptions, which if unresolved could spoil a good relationship.

1. *Misconception* – **'If I work hard I will be loved.'**
   Emotion – **Anxiety, discouragement, rejection.**
   Behaviour – **Perfectionism, hard work, overly helpful.**

At first glance Judy appears to be a very fortunate young woman. She is entertaining, helpful and always in demand. Her presence at a party makes it go with a swing. Her willingness to bake a cake, baby-sit or visit a sick person keeps her continually occupied and appreciated. How could anyone so popular ever feel depressed? Yet Judy not only gets depressed but she often feels suicidal. Her whirl of frantic activity is, in fact, a way of overcoming a deep sense of rejection. From somewhere inside her comes a message that she has no right to be alive. In an effort to overcome this feeling she tries to earn the right for existence. But she never fully succeeds in this. She always feels she has to do more.

An infant's feelings of self-worth are intrinsically tied in with his parents' view of him. His sense of value grows as he experiences his parents' evident enjoyment of his being. Judy apparently never sensed any such thing. She felt an unwanted, unwelcome baby and like any other infant in her place she unconsciously identified with rejection. She felt herself to be a dreadful mistake and the only way to make amends for inflicting society with her presence was to work hard and make herself necessary to others. Her thinking ran like this, 'If I work hard and make myself useful then people will be glad to have me around.'

This same message is also communicated to a child whose parents put a high value on achievement. A child who invariably receives praise and loving embraces for success but disapproval and the cold shoulder for failure will quickly deduce that to be acceptable he must succeed. This sort of person lives in a constant state of anxiety. He dreads making a mistake and feels it is the end of the world if he does.

A young man once came to see me, worried because he was about to be married and felt he could not go through with it. He was obviously very anxious. He assured me that he loved the young lady. She was approved of by the family. Like himself she was also a Christian and there seemed no reason why he should not marry her, except that he was afraid he could be making a terrible mistake. When we prayed together the Holy Spirit very quickly revealed the root of his problem. As a child he had been severely punished when he failed and he was rarely encouraged when he succeeded. From then on his life had become one agonising effort to get things right. But even when he did he was still never sure it would be acceptable.

A person with a deeply imbedded sense of rejection is either over-sensitive and constantly feels rejected by friends, or is always trying to prevent feared rejection by hard work. When this sort of anxiety is brought into a relationship the pleasure is spoiled. It is hard to relax with someone who constantly wants to please or is always needing reassurance.

For Consideration:
Do you have to work hard to make your friends love you?
Do you worry that your friends may lose interest in you?
Can you totally relax with any of your friends?

2. *Misconception* – 'I am responsible for other people's happiness.'
   Emotion – Insecurity, depression, anger, guilt.
   Behaviour – Controls, takes responsibility, care-takes and rescues others.

A dysfunctional family may be one which lives in permanent chaos. Its members fight, they cry, they are late for everything, they owe money, they don't wear the right clothes for the right occasions, they forget homework and parents' evenings. Children in this sort of family live with constant insecurity. Sometimes one child, most probably the oldest, tries to put some order into the family. She starts remembering appointments, gets the younger ones dressed in the mornings, does the shopping and so on. With a little bit of order comes a sense of security and everyone is happier. All thanks to the super-responsible oldest child.

Perhaps a mother or father was alcoholic or for some reason not able to cope well with life. The child may take up the job of parenting the parent. In both these cases the parents allow the child to exercise the responsibility and then expect her to be responsible for keeping the family happy. She, in turn, accepts the challenge and in her immature mind takes on a life-commitment and then applies it in every relationship.

Andy is a care-taker and rescuer. He has enormous energy and enjoys organising. He organises his family, his home, his work, but it doesn't stop there. He seeks to organise any and everyone he has contact with. He can't ask anyone to do the smallest job for him without checking to see if he is doing it right and in the end probably does it himself because he thinks he can do it better. He rescues his friends and even acquaintances before they even realise they were in need of help. He does it with the best of intentions and cannot understand why his friends sometimes get irritated with him. Some accept it readily and grow lazy. They soon begin to expect him to be there whenever they need him, which he usually is. Unfortunately when Andy sometimes gets over-tired he feels that he is being taken advantage of and feels angry. Behind the controlling, rescuing adult hides a once very insecure little boy whose father had had a nervous breakdown from which he never fully recovered. Andy was the oldest child and gradually took over his father's place in the family. He comforted his mother and organised the younger ones. His efforts brought some welcome security and order back to the family who began to feel safer; so too did Andy! Thirty years later he is a compulsive controller and care-taker.

Melody Beattie, a recovering alcoholic and former chemical-dependency counsellor, identifies this type of controlling person as co-dependent and she spells out their rationale – a kind of co-dependent creed:

We control in the name of love.

We do it because we're 'only trying to help'.

We do it because we know best how things should go and how people should behave.

We do it because we're right and they're wrong.

We control because we're afraid not to.

We do it because we don't know what else to do.

We do it to stop the pain.

We control because we think we have to.

We control because we don't think.

We control because controlling is all we can think about.

Ultimately we may control because that's the way we've always done things.[1]

Being friends with a care-taker and rescuer has many advantages. Unfortunately it can also be very inhibiting at times. Such a person tends to take control of the friendship and take over the friend. He does things for the friend which the friend could easily do for himself. In so doing he may cause the friend either to feel annoyed or to abdicate responsibility and take advantage of the care-taker. When a close relationship develops between a strong rescuer and a helpless, needy individual then the friendship soon becomes an unhealthy, stagnant affair in which there is little room for growth and change.

Describing the rescuer Melody Beattie says that he not only meets people's needs he even anticipates them. He fixes, nurtures and fusses over others. He makes others feel better, he solves, attends to, and does it all so well. But later he gets angry and feels used and sorry for himself.[2]

Because co-dependency is an insidious trap and one which is easily mistaken for godliness we shall examine it in more detail in a further chapter.

For Consideration:
Do you feel compelled to help people solve their problems?
Do you feel happier giving to others than receiving from them?
Do you feel attracted to needy people?
Do you feel used sometimes?

3. *Misconception* – **'It is unbearable to be alone.'**
   Emotion – **Insecurity, anxiety, fear, inner emptiness.**
   Behaviour – **Dependence on others, clinginess, attention-seeking.**

   A new-born baby only 'exists' in relation to its mother. Too much enforced separation could nudge a baby to the 'edge of the abyss of non-being, trembling through the phase of separation-anxiety, eventually to fall, in a moment of horror, over the edge into nothingness, into the abandonment of hope, love, desire for life and expectation of access to humanity'.[3] Such an excruciating process may leave a baby with permanent emotional scarring. Even for an older child separation from mother, the source of nurture and comfort, or father, the source of protection and security, can leave a child with a nagging worry about any kind of future separations. The child grows up with a firm belief that to be left will cause unbearable suffering.

   Describing a person with a fear of separation, the psychiatrist, Dr Frank Lake writes, 'The panic-stricken baby is buried alive in the mind. It is as alive twenty, forty, sixty years later as at the moment of repression.' He goes on to explain that though the dread of separation may seem perpetually imminent this dread can be kept at bay so long as attention-seeking behaviour is maintained. 'Everything is sacrificed to the clamant emotional need for someone to cling to.'[4]

   Obviously when this sort of need is manifested in a friendship it can become very unhealthy. Everyone has some dependency needs. Few of us were nurtured perfectly and within us there will be a residue of unmet needs. However, when the meeting of these needs becomes the controlling

factor in a relationship the friendship will soon find itself in
trouble. Exclusivity, jealousy and possessiveness are usually
the outcome. Unfortunately dependency is not a rare occurrence in a friendship and because the implications are
significant we shall examine this problem also in a later
chapter.

For Consideration:
Do you look to your friends for security?
Can you enjoy an evening on your own?
Have you experienced feelings of jealousy and possessive-
ness in your friendships?

4. *Misconception* – **'Conflict is wrong. I must keep the
   peace at all costs.'**
   Emotion – **Fear, tension, anxiety, stress, insecurity.**
   Behaviour – **Avoids confrontation, suppresses angry
   feelings, leaves problems unresolved.**
   Much childhood learning comes through modelling. A
child observes his parents doing things and learns as he
watches. A mother and father whose only method of resolving conflict is to come to blows and scream at one another
are communicating a message that conflict is bad. Every
time the child hears arguments or raised voices his heart
will beat faster with fear. Too many children have had the
experience of lying in bed at night with their heads under
the pillow and fingers in their ears trying to block out the
angry shouts and screams of rowing parents. An opposite
unhealthy model comes from parents who suppress their
feelings and teach the children to do the same. In such a
home conflict is never allowed, let alone resolved.
   When Maggie married Alan she was quite unprepared
for what ensued. On several occasions in the early weeks
of their marriage Alan became angry. He banged the pots
and pans around and raised his voice. Poor Maggie was
ill-equipped to cope with such an experience. Her father
was an upright, Christian man, who had never raised his
voice to her mother and had not allowed his children to

show anger or strong emotion of any kind. Maggie grew up to be an habitual suppressor of feelings and was under the misconception that her manner of handling her bad feelings was much more 'Christian' than her husband's way. She would pussy-foot around Alan trying not to upset him and studiously avoided topics of conversation which might cause friction. Consequently after many years of married life no areas of conflict had ever been resolved. Alan was incredibly frustrated and she was constantly anxious.

At the other end of the scale the Masons fought daily. Plates would fly whilst angry blows and words would be exchanged. Rose Mason once turned up on my door-step with a black-eye, given her by her husband Tony. Sadly it was the children who showed the stress of living in such turmoil. They did badly at school and on several occasions were caught stealing.

In both these families the children received no model for dealing with conflict in a healthy way. Maggie now avoids conflict because it is alien to her. The children in the Mason family are already showing an angry response and in the future will most likely resort to the same harmful habits as their parents.

When two individuals relate as friends it is not because they are as alike as two peas in a pod. They may have some common interests but they each come from distinct and separate home backgrounds and will have different ideas and habits. Some tensions are bound to arise which need to be brought out into the open and talked through. Resentment may accrue towards a partner and this needs to be expressed in an appropriate manner but not by a loss of temper, nor by avoiding confrontation but by owning the bad feelings and seeking a time for discussion when these can be aired and a resolution found.

For Consideration:
How did your parents resolve problems?
Are you afraid of conflict?
Do you struggle to keep peace at all costs?

5. *Misconception* – 'A real friend intuits one's needs and puts one first.'
   Emotion – Disappointment, anger.
   Behaviour – Withdrawing, sulking.

Friendship does not necessarily make people clairvoyant. It is unreal to expect one's friend to know one's needs before they are expressed. Such a false expectation can only lead to disappointment and a stressed relationship.

A child who has felt neglected because of her parents' excessive preoccupation with someone or something else, may have harboured some very angry thoughts and feelings. She may have had five or six years being the 'only child' and then along came a new baby and mother and father became very preoccupied with it. The child thinks, '"They" ought to know what I am feeling. After all "they" are supposed to love me.' At this stage a demand to have her needs met spontaneously by her parents takes root. To ask for it, or to express it would, to her immature mind, diminish the value of their response. She feels that the response has to be spontaneous or it is not worth having. When these feelings are never properly resolved they can be transferred later to a friend or spouse who will be totally unaware of such expectations.

Another root cause of such an unreasonable demand could lie within a person whose normal, but temporary, need to be 'omnipotent' in the early months of life was never fully satisfied. Babies are born with an instinctive expectation that their needs will be met on demand. It is only a phase and gradually this expectation diminishes and the ability to cope with disappointment develops. This is aided by the presence of older children or the arrival of another baby. It could be that this unmet infantile need is still latent within the adult and only re-emerges with the stimulation of a close relationship.

Friendship often involves disappointment. The friend can forget a birthday, or be late for a date. He can overlook the signs of tiredness or sadness and fail to give the correct or expected response. At one time or another in every relationship this sort of thing will occur because friends are human and not infallible.

During our seventeen years in Chile we moved house frequently. It was always a strain, because so much would need doing to get the family resettled and David could only give a limited amount of time to helping with that. Usually others would help out and we would eventually get straight. However, on one particular house-moving we were well organised and left the children to spend the afternoon and evening with school friends. We agreed to pick them up at bed time. Unfortunately we were so busy that when David left to attend an evening meeting in one of the churches I forgot that I needed the car to fetch the children. I didn't panic because our closest friend lived near-by and I knew she would willingly fetch them once she had arrived. I was expecting her to come around to give me a hand with unpacking. I waited and waited but she never came. It was getting late and I knew the children should be in bed. Eventually I rang her house only to be told she had gone to bed. I was furious. 'How could she go to bed,' I thought, 'she knows how much I have to do.' I did eventually resolve the problem with the girls but the hurt that my friend had not realised how much I needed her did not subside. When she came around the next day I felt very cool! Even when I learned that she had suffered a migraine the night before it didn't eradicate the thoughts that if she had been a 'real friend' she would have put me first or at least rung and told me she wasn't coming. I was filled with disappointment and self-pity caused by my unreal expectations of friendship.

Since that time I have learned that, like me, my friends are not supermen or women. I know there will be occasions when they will disappoint me, but there are many other occasions when they will come up trumps and be there when I need them; read my mind; sense my mood; and remember my birthday! The good times far outweigh the disappointments.

For Consideration:
Do you expect your friends to be clairvoyant and just
'know' how you feel and what you need?
Do your friends disappoint you often?
Do you find it hard to forgive your friends when they let
you down?

   The above beliefs and the feelings that accompany them
can undoubtedly spoil a friendship. You may have identified with one of the hindrances or blockages we have
mentioned and are wondering how you can get rid of it.
As we have already said, acknowledging that you have a
problem and understanding why you have one are the first
steps in making the necessary changes. Healing any wounds
left over from childhood and the work of changing attitudes
and behaviour will follow. Before we examine this process
we need to mention other tendencies which can threaten a
potentially good relationship.

6

THE TRAP OF EMOTIONAL DEPENDENCY

King David in his early years experienced a close and loyal friendship with King Saul's son Jonathan. He also experienced the devastation of being betrayed by other close friends. 'They imagine the worst for me . . . even my close friend, whom I trusted.'[1] Then speaking of another, or perhaps the same friend, he says, 'If an enemy were insulting me, I could endure it . . . But it is you . . . my companion, my close friend.'[2] Maybe he passed on these experiences of both noble and ignoble friendship to his son Solomon. King Solomon had many good things to say about friendship but adds his own caution. 'A righteous man is cautious in friendship, but the way of the wicked leads them astray.'[3] God warns us that, 'The heart is deceitful above all things and beyond cure. Who can understand it?'[4] We are so often ignorant of what is really in our hearts. It is this lack of awareness which so easily leads us astray. One of the traps in friendship is that of emotional dependency.

In my role as a counsellor I have been called upon to listen to many horror stories from people who have enthusiastically initiated a friendship only to find themselves marooned on the muddy banks of dependency. Tearfully they have told their story of a promising friendship which has become increasingly unmanageable. Either both feel guilty at their growing need for intimacy or one feels rejected and the other drained by the unreasonable demands for love and attention.

Looking at the insidious trap of dependency you may
well say to yourself, as too many have done before you,
'It could never happen to me.' But the heart is deceitful and when emotions are touched, unmet needs, buried
hurts and unsatisfied longings may well be stirred up too.
These can easily catch a person unawares and before the
brakes can be applied he is enmeshed in a painful trap from
which he is only freed with difficulty.

Having unmet needs is a fairly normal state of affairs for
most people. However, if friendship is used to meet those
needs difficulties will follow. Andy Comiskey, who in the
past was a practising homosexual and is now a married
man with four children, writes with great understanding
and insight about the problems of emotional dependency.
He describes the desperation within many for the strong
arms of a father or the safe breast of a mother. Such a
basic human need is not sinful. But when this yearning for
a father or a mother becomes the motivating factor in our
adult relationships, we can easily fall into a disordered state.
He warns us that such unmet needs may seem to compel
us to bow down at the altar of 'false parents'. We may
be adults with some childish needs, but we can own that
reality without attempting to make another human being
the parent that he or she is not.[5]

None of us are totally free of the danger of becoming
dependent. However, there are those for whom the need to
depend is like a gnawing ache. Such a person's inner pain
cries out to be alleviated by someone warm and strong
and she is drawn like a magnet to a parental person. She
finds aloneness intolerable and feels empty and incomplete without someone there specially for her. A mature
friendship is unlikely to develop out of what must be an
inevitably shallow alliance. It may appear to be an intense
relationship but most such emotionally needy people are
too self-absorbed, too hungry for love to provide the input
necessary for true friendship to grow.

Even in a friendship where neither partner is aware
of having abnormal dependency-needs such feelings could

surface and catch both of them unawares. Family circumstances may have encouraged a child to suppress normal
needs for nurture, love, touch and comfort. Suppression,
however, does not mean that these needs disappear. Having
lain dormant and unrecognised within a person for many
years they can be stimulated by a close relationship and
suddenly surface taking the friends by surprise.

John Powell suggests that buried emotions are rather
like rejected people; they tend to make us pay a high
price for having rejected them. In fact hell hath no fury
like that of a scorned emotion.[6]

Realising the danger is the first step in avoiding the trap
of dependency. The next one is being able to recognise
the type of relationship which would correspond to this
label. The following list of elements found in a dependent
relationship should help us to do this. Once we know what
we are dealing with the best antidote is honesty: honesty
with ourselves and before God. We need to ask God to
search us out and show us our hearts and our thoughts; to
see if there is any offensive way in our relationships and if
so to lead us in a better way.[7]

Elements to be Found in Emotionally Dependent Relationships

Jealousy and Possessiveness

Most friendships are from time to time beset by the difficult
feelings of jealousy and possessiveness. When these are recognised, confessed to God and repented of, the storm can be
weathered fairly easily. However, if it is a recurring problem
which surfaces in every close relationship it is symptomatic
of deeper emotional problems which could be helped by
some counselling. In the case of a person who suffers
occasional feelings of jealousy, to understand the cause will
often be sufficient to disperse the feelings. Remember that
God has known us since we were in our mother's womb[8]
and will reveal the truth to us if we ask Him.

Several years ago while on holiday with some close friends

a mutual acquaintance was mentioned. Our friends began
to describe this lady in glowing terms. The more euphoric
they became the more silent I became. I could feel some
distinctly uncomfortable feelings stirring within me. As I
asked God what these feelings were about I remembered
experiencing the same sensations on a previous occasion.
This episode happened many years ago in Chile when David
had attended a supper party at one of the English chap-
laincy churches. He had met a lady there who later became a
close friend of the family. But at the time she was unknown
to either of us. On returning home he sang her praises to me
because she had had such a friendly and lively personality.
At the time I was trying to cope with four tiny children and
feeling decidedly jaded, so did not appreciate his enthusiasm. That memory gave me the clue to why I was now, many
years later, experiencing similar discomfort. My low self-
esteem had caused me to compare myself very unfavourably
with the, then unknown, lady. Now I was threatened in
much the same way. I was forgetting the understanding,
trust, intimacy and commitment, both with David and with
these friends, which had developed over the years. These
are lasting qualities in a relationship and are not easily
destroyed. But momentarily I had lost sight of the truth.

Exclusivity

Left to smoulder and grow, jealousy and possessiveness can
become very manipulative elements in a friendship and can
lead on to exclusivity. Other people are viewed as a threat.
Neither partner feels free to invite others to join them for an
outing or a meal and certainly neither seems free to spend
time alone with any other friend.

When a friendship has become exclusive, others quickly
get the message that they are in the way. Meaningful
looks are exchanged which make them feel uncomfortable
and effectively shut them out. I remember the first time I
ever met this type of exclusive relationship. I was a new
missionary and longed to make friends with the rest of
the missionary team working in the area. I took on the

job of becoming the missionary postwoman. Every day I would collect the letters from the little post office and deliver them round our missionary hospital and school. It gave me an opportunity to stop and have a chat with folk. Mostly I received a welcome and often a cup of tea. But whenever I went to one place I was thoroughly embarrassed and made a quick exit. Two lady missionaries would nearly always be deep in conversation together. They were oblivious of everyone else and my arrival seemed an unwelcome intrusion. Their friendship had become an exclusive one which effectively shut others out.

Lack of Freedom

Exclusivity quickly gives rise to a lack of freedom. True love is liberating not imprisoning. It offers a person roots, that is, a sense of belonging, as well as wings, that is, a sense of freedom.[9] When the relationship becomes exclusive there is no freedom to grow. Nor is there the independence necessary to be a person in one's own right. Togetherness is an important element but so too is separateness. Bought plants these days are usually accompanied with instructions to bed them out a certain distance apart. This will give freedom for their roots to spread. As they grow they may appear at first rather too separate but the more room the roots have the stronger the plants will be and eventually they will become big enough to touch each other without any damage occurring. Without freedom a friendship chokes to death.

Enmeshment

This phenomenon is frequently found in twins, especially identical twins. Fraternal twins or siblings close in age may also demonstrate the same tendency. Sometimes it occurs within a close marriage relationship. Within a friendship the exclusivity and togetherness we have already mentioned may lead on to a degree of unhealthy psychical (soul or mind) fusion. It usually occurs when mental and emotional boundaries are not respected and the people concerned begin to flow in and out of each other's personality. It is heady and exciting to find oneself so close to another human being that each knows what the other is thinking and feeling. However, ego boundaries are necessary to our mental, emotional and spiritual health and when they are crossed it is a violation of the personality. When indulged in too much for too long it can lead to mental breakdown or even oppression from Satan. It is as if the normal, God-given protection around our 'innermost being' has been rent.

In a recent edition of the *Sunday Telegraph* there was a reproduction of a fascinating series of paintings which expressed acute mental turmoil. Bryan Charnley was the artist. He tragically committed suicide at the age of forty-one just after painting the pictures. The paper reported his case history. Bryan had a twin brother, Terence, who survived him. Though they were not identical twins, as they grew up they were emotionally enmeshed and dependent upon one another. They communicated with each other in a private language and each knew what the other was thinking. However, when they were at secondary school Terence felt the need to break away from his brother. He began to hate being a part of a double act called 'The Charnley Twins'. Their mother traced many of Bryan's subsequent problems back to Terence's attempt to sever the bonds of being a twin. At eighteen Bryan had his first breakdown and until his death twenty-three years later fought a daily battle with mental illness.[10]

Fantasising and Daydreaming
This is another characteristic of a dependent relationship. Time is spent daydreaming and imagining opportunities for increased closeness and intimacy. These fantasies activate a hunger for greater demonstrations of love. This could lead on to a heightened need for more physical affection.

Physical Intimacy
Touch is vital for our physical health and between close friends it can be very restorative, relaxing and even healing.

But when physical intimacy becomes an intense and habitual part of a friendship there is always a danger of crossing the boundaries of what is correct. There may be no previous homosexual experience in the lives of either partner. Both may believe themselves to be completely heterosexual. Nevertheless inappropriate intimacy can occur when there is an infantile need for nurture and touch which has never been sufficiently met in childhood. When satisfaction for those needs is actively sought a sexual arousal may follow. Whether we like it or not we are all sexual beings. These feelings have an addictive quality to them and once roused are hard to control. When physical intimacy goes too far the cause is usually to be found in naïveté and ignorance, which I hope this chapter will disperse; or in an arrogant self-confidence that has taken no heed of the warning signs. Normally, being aware of the dangers is all that is needed to keep demonstrations of affection within safe limits.

Compensation
This is another component sometimes found in dependent relationships. It is quite common to find an extremely macho man married to a seemingly delicate female. She carries his feminine attributes for him and he carries her masculine ones. Though a man should be thoroughly masculine and a woman truly feminine, both should be able to enjoy and experience some opposite-sex characteristics which enhance and enrich their personalities. We are made in God's image. He is revealed in Scripture as having both masculine and feminine attributes. Therefore we are in our spiritual, psychological and physical beings – bipolar creatures. 'The more nearly we function in His image, the more nearly we reflect both the masculine and the feminine in their proper balance – that is, in the differing degrees and aptitudes appropriate to our sexual identities as male and female.'[11] Some races and families particularly discourage any femininity being expressed by their male population and any masculine attributes being expressed by the

women. They then compensate by marrying a person who will carry the traits they have rejected in themselves. This tends to lock the couple into static roles and can be very inhibiting for growth and change. A person made in the image of God should be developing and growing over the years and increasingly manifesting a rounded personality.

This type of compensation can also be a part of same-sex friendships. For example, a decisive and orderly person may become close friends with a spontaneous and flexible person. Fear of losing control most likely inhibits him from expressing those qualities himself. By close association with a person who has them in abundance he is able to avoid the challenge of changing. He will relax and let his friend express those qualities for him.

Cannibal Compulsion

Yet another aspect of compensation is what Leanne Payne calls the 'cannibal compulsion'. This is frequently to be found within the homosexual. A missionary once told Leanne that, 'Cannibals eat only those they admire, and they eat them to get their traits.'[12] They believe that by devouring such a person they will then possess those coveted attributes. A homosexual has rejected a part of himself: by uniting with a person he perceives as having the quality he lacks he may incorrectly believe he will regain that lost part.

Financial Commitment

Lastly a dangerous temptation for an emotionally enmeshed relationship is to bind it with a financial commitment. Within dependent relationships hides a deep insecurity. The evidence for this is seen in the possessiveness and lack of freedom which is experienced in most cases. Financial commitment, usually in the form of buying a house together, is embarked upon with the hope that it will minimise this insecurity, and overcome the fear of loss. Sadly it rarely succeeds. But it does succeed in creating a strong tie that so easily becomes a bondage and a cause for manipulation. A financial commitment should only be entered into after serious thought and prayer as to its true motivation and with legal advice and help. Nothing should be signed without the full understanding that either party can withdraw at any time.

For many single people their only hope of buying a house is to do so in conjunction with a friend. In fact David and I have been part of such a scheme with a long-standing friend. Even though we knew each other well and felt able to trust one another, we nevertheless took the precaution of having a solicitor draw up the agreement with the necessary clauses to make it safe for all of us.

Yes but-ery!

Having read these pages you may find yourself saying, 'Yes! But . . .'

Can anything be wrong with my relationship if I feel so close to God in it?

There may be nothing wrong with your relationship. However, feelings are not the plumb-line by which to measure it. Where our emotions are involved it is very easy to be deceived. When praying with our friend we may feel closer to God than ever before. However, emotional feelings should not be mistaken for spirituality. A spiritual experience may involve the emotions but that does not make it more spiritual. An emotional experience may feel spiritual but have very little to do with God. Emotional entanglement with another person is heady stuff and can waft us into a spiritual euphoria. Needs for love, comfort and nurture are being met. The heart is warmed and melted. It may indeed feel like a taste of heaven!

Another 'Yes but . . .' is, *Why shouldn't I have my needs met? Others do.*

The problem with a very close, dependent relationship is that it tends to meet these needs superficially and temporarily and in the process takes the edge off one's hunger for God.

Through the prophet Jeremiah, God showed his disappointment with His people because instead of turning to Him to meet their needs they had turned to men or idols. Jeremiah spelt out God's response, 'Cursed is the one who trusts in man, who depends on flesh for his strength and whose heart turns away from the Lord.'[13] 'My people have exchanged their Glory for worthless idols.'[14] He accuses his people of two sins. In the first place they have forsaken Him, and then dug their own wells, broken wells that cannot hold water.[15] In other words instead of looking to Him as their major source of satisfaction and comfort, they had expended their energies devising other ways to meet those needs.

In the end these self-made means never satisfy. In fact in God's eyes they are idolatrous. 'Idolatry can be defined as filling our need for love with something or someone God has made rather than with God Himself.'[16] A young girl spoke to me at a conference recently in great distress. She had become friendly with an older woman. Now she was obsessed with thoughts of her and had even started dreaming about her. 'I can't help it,' she said. 'I want to be with her all the time.' This lack of will-power and compulsiveness is frequently the sign of a dependent relationship and it is also a mark of idolatry. 'But you said, "It's no use! I love foreign gods, and I must go after them." '[17]

When anyone has missed out on maternal nurture or paternal affirmation it leaves an aching void behind. Once the years of infancy are over the chance to be nurtured or affirmed within such close dependency has passed. It is no longer possible to receive such undivided attention. Only God, our Eternal Father, can bind up our broken hearts and fill our emptiness. All substitutes will fail. We may think our friend will make up the deficiency but unfortunately he or she will just activate the hunger which makes us want more. The hunger is insatiable until God mends our brokenness and satisfies our deepest longings with Himself. But God requires our attention and our time in order to do this for us. Only in His presence, as we wait upon Him and worship Him, will this healing gradually happen. A young man in the process of breaking free from homosexuality told me that the most significant factor in his own healing was the time he spent worshipping and praying in tongues.

For Consideration:
Do you have needs for love and comfort which you are meeting through means other than God?
Are the following characteristics present in any of your friendships?
    Jealousy
    Possessiveness
    Exclusivity
    Lack of freedom
    Enmeshment
    Fantasising and daydreaming
    Inappropriate physical intimacy
    Compensation
    A financial commitment

Emotional dependency is a trap which this chapter may help you avoid. However, some may read it and feel that they are already ensnared and are wondering how to break free.

Breaking Free
Coming out of denial is the first step and if you have already admitted to yourself that you are trapped in a dependent relationship you are part-way to breaking free. The next step is to *confess your sins to God*. Preferably *in front of another person*. James exhorts us to confess our sins to one another and to pray for one another so that we may be healed.[18] Choose a mature person who will not be shocked by your confession, but be sure you make a clean breast of it. Do not be tempted to skirt over the details. As we speak aloud what has actually occurred we come to hate the sin: this strengthens our will to flee from it. Having acknowledged the trap one has fallen into, it is then necessary to *extricate*

oneself from it. Breaking off the relationship completely may not be possible, or advisable. However, there has to be a definite 'emotional separation', which is only achieved through painful self-denial. This will mean denying oneself those things which previously fed the dependence, such as the exclusivity, the fantasising and the excessive amount of time spent together. Unhealthy dependence will not just die of its own accord; it has to be starved to death.

Coming out of denial, confessing our sins and practising self-discipline will go a long way to protecting us from future entanglements. However, there were underlying reasons why you became ensnared by dependency in the first place. The next step is to seek healing. Our unhealed hurts and unmet needs will continue to trap us until they are dealt with.

Traps are only traps because they are well-hidden and catch us unawares. Others are therefore worth exposing before we move on to the more positive aspects of friendship.

THE TRAP OF CO-DEPENDENCY

The term co-dependency is a recent addition to the therapist's vocabulary, though it is not new to their experience. It has also become an increasingly popular subject on the pop-psychology bookshelves in recent years.

Originally the term was reserved for people who had a close relationship to a chemically (alcohol or drugs, etc.) dependent person. They were seen as 'partners in dependency'. The spouse or friend of an alcohol or drug abuser would often develop an unhealthy way of coping with the situation and this was known as co-dependent behaviour. Gradually the term was expanded to include any person who co-operated in sustaining any type of unhealthy dependency upon another. Currently the term seems to have broadened out even further and can be defined as, 'An addiction to people, behaviour, or things. Co-dependency is the fallacy of trying to control interior feelings by controlling people, things and events on the outside. To the co-dependent, control or the lack of it is central to every aspect of life.'[1] It would therefore seem to embrace not only those who are addicted, but also those who are addicted to helping the addicted!

The trap of co-dependency within friendship is quite subtle and sometimes hard to distinguish from loving care. Jason is someone who contacts me infrequently but always urgently. He wants me to advise him on how to sort out the problem belonging to a close friend, who may be a total stranger to me. He rarely rings me about himself but only about the needs of others. His life revolves around other

people's problems. Lame ducks are attracted to Jason and
Jason is drawn like a magnet to them. In relationships
Jason shows all the marks of co-dependency, but would
call it 'love'. Actually he is obsessed with other people's
problems, and fits Melody Beattie's description of a co-
dependent exactly. 'A person who has let another person's
behaviour affect him or her, and who is obsessed with
controlling that person's behaviour.'[2]

A co-dependent is unaware that his friendships are unhealthy. He sees himself as some sort of saviour, called
to rescue, help, make better his 'dear friend'. The 'dear
friend's' problem becomes the co-dependent's problem. He
takes over his 'dear friend's' life in an effort to control the
problem for him. On the surface it appears very loving, sac-
rificial behaviour. In fact it is a compulsive and obsessional
need to relate to troubled people. A co-dependent is dependent upon solving other people's problems.

This is not to decry sacrifice and service for others which
is part of the Christian commitment. It is simply to say
that a co-dependent is not actually doing this primarily to serve Christ but to meet his own deep insatiable
needs.

Being without sin Jesus was godly in all his relationships,
yet he related to many troubled people. But he was able,
at times, to say 'no' to their demands in order to spend
time alone with his Heavenly Father or with his friends.
It is recorded that He even moved on although the sick
were still calling for him in the place where he had been.[3]
Jesus did nothing to please himself. His delight was to do
what pleased his Father.[4] He was neither manipulated
nor obsessed by troubled people, yet out of compassion,
and in obedience to his Father's will, gave his life for
them. His followers, down through the ages, have done
likewise. Mother Teresa of Calcutta is probably the best-
known modern-day example of a life sacrificed for the
poor and needy. This should not be confused with the
behaviour of a co-dependent.

The underlying misconceptions of a co-dependent – 'I am

*responsible for . . .' 'It's up to me to put her right,' 'He will
fall apart without me.'*
   The two main emotions – Guilt, anxiety.
   *The behaviour – To look after, to take responsibility for,
and to rescue troubled people.*

The Causes of Co-dependency

The root cause of co-dependency, as already mentioned,
comes out of a person's formative years spent within a
dysfunctional family system. However, there are several
factors in particular which could cause a person to become
co-dependent.

Conditional Love

One of the factors seems to be conditional love which was
meted out in childhood. A home where affection is tied in
to performance and where nothing a child does is ever quite
good enough sows the seeds of perfectionism within the
heart of a child. Quite unconsciously an idea is formulated
that the secret to being loved and accepted depends upon
being what others want you to be. The child then grows up
to be a people-pleaser. She learns to be always there for
others, never for herself; always ready to 'do' for others
things she would never spend time on doing for herself.

A lady I know was in a bad way emotionally and physically but could not bring herself to ask for prayer. 'I can't
bother people,' she would say. Then one day her close
friend became very sick and immediately the lady was
asking people to pray for her friend. She did not mind
'bothering' others on behalf of her friend but never for
herself. Such a person's life gradually comes to revolve
around making other people happy. 'If I can make him or
her happy, then at last I will have got it right.'

Lucy grew up in a home where nothing she ever did
pleased her father. Conditional love was the only love she
ever knew from him. 'If I am good, if I am tidy, if I do
well, Daddy will love me.' This was the conviction that
controlled her childhood behaviour. Now many years later

she lives her life to please others and meet their needs. She sacrifices many hours for other people. She misses meals to run their errands. She works extra hours to cover up their mistakes. In Lucy's case her co-dependency grew out of a need to be loved and accepted by her father.

Inner Pain

Another factor which can produce co-dependency is inner pain. Emotional discomfort can be handled in several different ways. Some emotionally healthy people will express their feelings to an appropriate person and be open to God's healing. Others may simply curl up and sleep, hoping it will go away. Another will ease his own pain by finding someone else with a similar pain and make him feel better. I know a man who felt very abandoned as a child. Today he has enormous patience and time for children who were hurt like himself. He gives to them what he never received himself. This partially eases his own inner pain. It is as if he is able to love his own 'inner child' through loving other abandoned children. Yet another person will handle his pain by totally focusing on other people. Everything but the other person's problems are forgotten including his own discomfort. The latter two ways of handling inner pain are the behaviour of a co-dependent. In many instances this help will be of great benefit to the one helped. The danger is that a person's own unhealed inner pain may cloud his judgment. He is then not able to discern how much, how long and what type of help it is wise to offer. Only when the motivating factor for giving help is the other person's well-being and happiness is the helper's discernment pure and unclouded.

Repetition

'We all possess a primal need to recreate the familiar, the original family situation, even if the familiar, the situation, is destructive and painful.'[5] It is this need to recreate the nostalgic familiar that will drive the child of an alcoholic father to marry a man who is, or who has, the tendencies for becoming an alcoholic. It is a totally unconscious drive.

She is completely surprised and upset when she discovers what has happened. The poor woman then spends years embroiled in her husband's addiction. Trying to hide it, trying to control it and trying to cure it. As the graffiti writer has said so wisely, 'There is no future in nostalgia.'

By recreating the familiar a person also gives himself a second chance. The daughter of the alcoholic who marries an alcoholic gives herself a second chance to make it better. 'This time I will fix it,' she hopes.

A child who was tormented by a parent's bad behaviour may also have a desperate desire to control that behaviour and make it right for the whole family. This obsession to 'make it right' for everyone may continue for the rest of her life and affect all her relationships.

Characteristics of a Co-dependent Relationship

Though a co-dependent relationship may have the symptoms of other disordered ways of relating, certain characteristics are particularly pertinent to a co-dependent friendship.

Problem-based

One of the marks of co-dependent friendships is that one partner is 'troubled' and the other takes responsibility for solving the problem. The relationship is formed around the problem and the co-dependent partner lives his life through his friend; making great sacrifices for him; obsessed with his friend and his friend's problem.

Dramatic

Another feature is that the friendship has a tendency to move from one drama to another. It seems to need the emotional upsets to keep the adrenalin flowing. From the outside it appears to be a disastrous partnership but in fact the melodrama has become addictive and is an important element in the relationship.

Intense and Obsessive

A good friendship can be filled with comfortable affection.

'Affection is an affair of old clothes, and ease, of the unguarded moment, of liberties which would be ill-bred if we took them with strangers.'[6] An affectionate relationship is also very relaxing and restful and therefore refreshing. 'No need to talk. No need to make love. No needs at all except perhaps to stir the fire.'[7]

The opposite would be true of a co-dependent friendship. These tend to be exhausting in their intensity. Both parties are obsessed and driven by the problem issues which cause intense emotions. The friendship is filled with demands and manipulations instead of relaxation and refreshment. The relationship is the major focus of their lives, whereas in a healthy friendship attention is given and time is spent on interests outside the relationship.

Mood Swings

Because the relationship is very enmeshed and intense the couple are tied into one another's moods. If the troubled partner is particularly unhappy the other works anxiously at making the unhappy partner happy. If this succeeds the mood changes and becomes euphoric.

Even in a good relationship one occasionally falls into the co-dependent trap. I love the sun, the beach and the sea. On holiday I like nothing more than to spend all day enjoying those luxuries. David, on the other hand, dislikes all three and will spend his days in the shade reading and writing. He emerges to buy a meal, a newspaper or to visit a place of interest. The first few days of every holiday I spend feeling guilty and worrying that David could be feeling abandoned. I dash back early from the beach to the hotel and suggest an outing, or something to eat. I want to be sure he is happy. But I am not by nature a co-dependent person and after a while I get tired of taking responsibility for David's holiday and leave him to pursue his own interests. Which of course he does very happily.

In a co-dependent relationship this never happens. The couple are so tied into each other that they live on an emotional see-saw. The troubled partner sets the mood. He falls into a pit of despair. The rescuer gets dragged into the gloom and tries to make it better. He succeeds and the partner starts to climb out. Both soar upwards. Until another problem takes over. It is an addictive, vicious cycle.

Guilt

Guilt haunts the co-dependent. This uncomfortable feeling drives or empowers the rescuing behaviour. If the underlying goals in life are to put things right, and to solve other people's problems, then failure will be a frequent outcome. Unfortunately, instead of bringing the co-dependent person to the realisation that his goals are unrealistic, the failure causes him to feel guilty and this guilt makes him try harder to succeed next time. The vicious cycle again.

Control

Control is a major issue for a co-dependent. He tries to control others for very good reasons. At least so he tells you. 'It's for their own protection.' 'It's for their own good.' 'So that they won't mess up their lives.' Or, 'It's just because I really do know best.' Controlling is manipulation and is done in many different ways. By moaning, by demanding, by anger, by crying, by whining, by cajoling and by threatening. All, of course, in the name of friendship and love. Insecurity would probably be a more honest explanation for the behaviour. To be out of control, or to have someone he loves be out of control, is a fearful prospect for a co-dependent.

A co-dependent relationship is not godly, nor healthy. It does not produce maturity in either partner. It is deceptive because it looks good and feels good. Few co-dependents realise what is the true motivation for their involvement in troubled people's lives. It is more in order to meet their own needs than to benefit the other person. For this reason we need to bring our relationships into the light and examine them, being prepared to ask ourselves some difficult questions.

For Consideration:
Have you related closely to many troubled people during your lifetime?
Are you relating closely to a troubled person at present?
Do you worry about this person's problem?
Do you feel responsible for solving it?
How would you feel if that person were not there for you to help?
Do you have a need to control people, things and situations?

If your answers are mainly in the affirmative you probably have some co-dependent tendencies in the way you relate to others. Because the motivation behind this behaviour is usually one of insecurity the next step will be to seek God's healing. However, before we consider the healing journey, we must look at one other trap which could ensnare those in search of real friendship.

OUT OF BOUNDS

In the Garden of Eden, Eve was deceived first by the serpent and then by her own desires. 'When the woman saw that the fruit of the tree was good for food and pleasing to the eye, and also desirable for gaining wisdom, she took some and ate it.'[1] God had already made it quite plain that the fruit of the tree of knowledge of good and evil was out of bounds to Adam and Eve. Every other fruit could be eaten but none from that tree. However, the fruit attracted Eve. She thought to herself that here was something which would satisfy her at every level of her being and would make her like God if she ate it.

In the forming of our friendships we are sometimes deceived into thinking that they must inevitably be healthy when they are not, as in emotional dependency or co-dependency. We can also be deceived into tasting forbidden fruit. The longing to have our needs satisfied will sometimes tempt us into a friendship with someone which is clearly forbidden fruit. When this happens, like Eve it does not just affect ourselves but others also. Adam was drawn into Eve's disobedience and the whole world was affected as a result. When we step outside the boundaries which God has clearly set around relationships we draw others into our sin. None of us live to ourselves. God has made us with the need and ability to relate to others. In most instances we would be quite free to take a new relationship on further into a richer friendship. Unfortunately our desires sometimes deceive us into taking unwise risks outside the God-given boundaries.

Throughout our lives we are accustomed to making relationships which exist at different levels of intimacy. These come into being perhaps for a specific purpose or in a particular situation. Within the limitations of that given purpose or situation they are right and proper. Only if both parties are free should the relationship ever move to a deeper level of intimacy.

I recently attended the wedding of a friend who was marrying her boss. The relationship began in the workplace but had gradually been taken further. They had both been free to develop their friendship. Had one of them been married it is hoped that the relationship would have remained limited to that of working partners and the emotional boundary between them maintained.

The novel, *How Green Was My Valley,* is rich with descriptions of human relationships. It is written through the eyes of Huw Morgan growing from childhood to manhood in a Welsh mining valley. After his brother Ivor is killed, Huw is sent to live with his sister-in-law Bronwen. He describes the emotional distance they carefully observed. 'There was a line drawn between us that was plain as though put there fresh with chalk every day. From each side of that line we lived, and spoke, and smiled . . . If we came near each other we were like hedgehogs with spines to keep away, though we never showed it. But we knew it.'[2]

Since situational boundaries are not always easy to maintain, it is wise to set ourselves emotional boundaries such as Huw and Bronwen set for themselves. Unfortunately these tend to be slightly nebulous so it is easy to ignore them. The boss and his married secretary, or the counsellor and his counsellee, could easily meet at a party. The situation may have changed but providing both keep within the emotional boundary all will be well. However, many people fail to observe this and even to realise there is any need to do so. A person may be lonely and in need of friendship but this does not give him permission to explore and develop every relationship. Only one in ten acquaintances may be suitable for close friendship.

Many situations present the opportunity for moving unwisely along the sliding scale of intimacy. One of these is the counselling room.

The Counselling Room

The relationship between a person who asks for help and the one who gives it should have quite clear demarcation lines. Unfortunately much of the Christian counselling which exists is rather haphazard and the boundaries are never clarified, nor implemented in any specific way.

Some Christians dislike, distrust and therefore disregard all secular counselling. When they do this they deny themselves the wisdom, accumulated over the years, which would help them avoid some of the pitfalls. Putting in boundaries and being answerable to a supervisor are very sensible secular practices which should be implemented by all counsellors.

I could cite many examples where this has not been done and tragedy has resulted. One was particularly sad because it affected so many other people. A married teacher was asked by one of his older female pupils if he would give her some counsel. He began to see her in a rather random way imagining it would only be a few sessions. However, she was a very needy young girl and he was a caring older man. The young pupil began to lean upon the teacher and he responded by giving her more time. Sometimes she would cry when he came to leave her and he would comfort her. No boundaries existed to give any protection to the relationship. Gradually her needs became more central to his life than those of his own family. Finally he left his wife, his children and his job to share his life with this very troubled girl.

Another similar case which did not have quite such a devastating outcome was between a pastor and a distressed girl in his care. The first mistake he made was to allow a very obvious boundary to be breached. He agreed to see this young girl late at night, alone, in the church office. He did not have the wisdom to recognise his vulnerability and to see the possible trap which lay ahead. The young lady arrived very upset and he tried to comfort her. Even in daytime this could be a dangerous moment in a counselling situation and for this reason one of the boundaries should be for men to avoid counselling women alone. In the instant the man stepped forward to comfort the girl he crossed the emotional boundary, which should have been his safeguard even when the situational one had broken down. She came into his arms and the damage was done. Very soon they were making love to one another. The experience for the man and the young woman was very painful but eventually God brought them both through to a place of forgiveness and healing. The girl sought help elsewhere. The man spent several weeks in an agony of guilt until he finally confessed and repented of his sin. He has since been restored to his ministry hopefully a much wiser man.

Besides prohibiting a man from counselling a woman on his own, another wise rule would be for every counsellor, male or female, to avoid ever counselling alone. When two counsellors are working together the situation of being shut up alone in a private place for an hour or more with a troubled and needy person is avoided. It is often difficult to maintain a physical distance when counselling, let alone an emotional one. In the beginning of my own counselling ministry no one told me about the dangers of counselling alone. On one occasion I was with a female counsellee in a room which was in a very isolated part of the church. We had been sitting opposite each other most of the time but at one point I drew my chair closer to pray for her. She began to cry as I prayed and suddenly she flung herself into my arms sobbing. I wasn't particularly worried at first, but then the way she clung to me made me feel quite uncomfortable and I tried to disentangle myself. In the middle of that experience I made my decision never to counsel on my own again. I had been considering asking someone to co-counsel with me and this finally decided me. I was not disturbed by my counsellee's expression of strong feeling. I was disturbed by the way in which she was obviously trying to meet her needs in me and by the memory of the growing list of sad stories I was receiving from people who had been caught and trapped in similar circumstances. One story had been an exact replica of my situation. A girl had fallen, crying, into the arms of her female counsellor. Only in her case the counsellor had responded too warmly and in a few moments erotic feelings were stirred and the two were involved in forbidden sexual intimacy.

Lori Thorkelson Rentzel's little book *Emotional Dependency* opens with the story of Mary and her counsellee Sarah. Both were Christians, both were married women and neither thought they had any homosexual tendencies. It therefore came as a shock when they found themselves emotionally and physically involved with each other.[3] When it comes to the hazards in a counselling relationship ignorance is not bliss, it is dangerous.

Another situational boundary which can be crossed in counselling without considering the strain it could incur, is co-counselling with a person of the opposite sex who is not one's spouse. Though many clergy seem to think they are safe enough to counsel alone in a closed room, some are aware of the dangers and look around for a person to co-counsel with. The most available person during the day may be someone other than his wife – the church warden's wife, or the lady deacon. This may start as a work relationship but it is hard in the emotionally charged environment of the counselling room and the debriefing after it to remain at a safe enough distance from one another. Confidentiality has to be maintained, therefore little can be shared with one's marriage partner. This inevitably means that the counsellors stay around and share together. Some feelings or memories may have been stirred within one of the counsellors and so one prays for the other. Communication at a deep level has been initiated. Before long a friendship develops which may easily undermine either's marriage relationship.

I have occasionally counselled alongside our supervisor, Richard Bedwell. It is very convenient to do so because he works in the church and is nearly always available. We have had a good work relationship for many years. We also have a good relationship as married couples as he works with David and I work with his wife Prue. Both the work relationship and the friendship have quite clear boundaries which we are both aware of. We may feel totally safe in both situations and would laugh at any suggestion of a greater involvement. Nevertheless we take the precaution of only co-counselling together on extremely rare, one-off occasions and then in a building where there is a lot going on and with the knowledge of our spouses. It would not be expedient to counsel together frequently for long hours even though it would be very convenient to do so. Emotional intimacy is built into such a relationship and neither of us is free to take such a risk.

Church Activities

Church activities offer opportunities for people to extend and deepen relationships. However, they also offer opportunities for people to be careless about boundaries.

During an evangelistic drive to reach unchurched folk in their parish one church decided to set up a programme of door to door visitation. For two evenings a week church members paired off and together called at houses in the parish. It was decided to pair off a man with a woman. In most instances only one member of a family was free to take up the challenge, which meant that in some cases a married man would accompany a married woman who was not his wife. Week by week these couples went from door to door. Sometimes their efforts were rewarded and they were invited in to share their faith. When this happened they were elated. At other times they were given a cool reception and felt dejected. At the end of their visiting they would spend time together talking over their experiences. In such circumstances the bounds of propriety can easily be crossed. Intimacy in this situation for one couple gradually developed into a romantic involvement. Normal boundaries are ignored at our peril.

It is also a sad fact that pastors often fail to implement safety precautions in their pastoral relationships and then find themselves in difficulty.

John White, author and psychiatrist, tells a salutary story of a Pastor Bill and a troubled lady called Joan. The case shows the subtle development of an innocent pastoral relationship. It started, quite faultlessly, with careful listening and comforting. It gradually developed into a sharing of mutual difficulties and as they prayed for one another they felt consoled. Out of this grew gratitude, respect, friendship and affection. The affection deepened and soon expressed itself physically.[4]

Even when, apparently, there seems to be no need to implement precautions in a pastoral situation, it is wise to remind oneself occasionally of the limitations which must naturally belong to a married person.

At separate conferences two women told me almost identical stories. Both were married to lay-men with some pastoral oversight in their local church. Recently, however, each man had become very friendly with another man in the church. In one case the relationship had begun through one man seeking advice from the other. Since then most evenings of the week the new friend was either ensconced in the husband's study or they spent the evening together in the other man's flat. They would talk together until late into the night and even occasionally into the early hours of the morning, while the wife sat alone. She knew, as did the other wife, that her company was not welcome and that she was excluded from the relationship. A deep intimate friendship had grown up through a normal pastoral concern.

The two ladies who spoke to me knew that their husbands were investing more emotional energy with their new friends than with them. These men had done nothing obviously wrong morally and yet anyone viewing the relationships would have queried the rightness of the situation.

Clergy wives particularly need to be reassured that their husbands' main emotional investment is with their families. The situational boundary between a pastor and his flock, or his staff, would be difficult to fix. He is obliged to meet with them in different places and at odd times. Several hours could be spent comforting a bereaved person. Many clergy do this without ever crossing the invisible boundary whereby they could become emotionally involved with another person. Their wives may be forced to spend many evenings alone but do so in the knowledge that their marriage is safe.

This opens up an important question. How much is a close friendship available to a married person outside of the marriage? Obviously between members of the opposite sex the situational and emotional boundaries should be set at a safe distance. However, between members of the same sex a friendship can be very enriching. Yet as we have seen, friendship, even between married people of the same sex, can be fraught with dangers. Boundaries, as always, are the key. Two important boundaries should be implemented. One limiting the amount of time spent in each other's company, and the other limiting the amount of physical affection shown to one another. For one partner to spend many hours exclusively in the company of another person has to be detrimental to a marriage. Also, though some people are very extrovert in their show of affection, I would suggest that frequent touching and hugging in private would be inappropriate, however harmless it may seem. Many people, especially women I have counselled, have become homosexually involved unintentionally. The friendship went wrong, as I have already illustrated, when quite innocently at first, they began to express their affection for one another physically and in private.

I recently talked with a man whose wife had just left both him and their daughter, to live with her best friend. The friendship began normally enough, but the two women had gradually begun to spend more and more time together alone. On one occasion, after a weekend together with her friend, the wife had confessed to some physical intimacy occurring, assuring her husband it wouldn't happen again. But the boundary had been crossed. Soon she was completely blinded to all other responsibilities and she left her husband to enter into a full-blown lesbian partnership.

May these regrettable illustrations serve only as a reminder of our human frailty and not as a deterrent from making friends. We need friendship and something with such rich potential should be protected. By staying within safe boundaries and observing certain precautions many of the above examples could have been avoided.

Safety Measures

The Bible says we should be 'as shrewd as snakes and as innocent as doves'.[5] I think this means that we must be wise about temptation and the attractions of evil, but that we should be innocent in our experience of sin. We are wise and will remain innocent when we 'stay always within the boundaries where God's love can reach and bless us'.[6]

1.   The first step then is to pray that God will indicate the appropriate boundaries for each new relationship.

2.   Secondly we must think ahead to the consequences of stepping outside these boundaries. Never be afraid to face the possible damage and destruction which could be wrought should lines be crossed.

I remember many years ago now taking a ride in a car with a fellow missionary. He had recently, like me, experienced a new release of the Holy Spirit in his life. It was before either my husband David or the missionary's wife had enjoyed such an experience. We had stopped the car and were engrossed in conversation when suddenly two disturbing thoughts crossed my mind. The first was a warning St. Paul gave to 'be careful to do what is right in the eyes of everybody'.[7] I realised that someone we knew, seeing us together, could easily draw the wrong conclusions. The second was about the consequences of crossing, even innocently, the previously well-defined limits of our relationship. Both thoughts appalled me. I quickly extricated myself from the situation. Wise people are doing this all the time.

3. Thirdly let's never be naive about our own capacity to sin however strong we may fancy ourselves to be. 'Pride goes before a fall' is a wise proverb. God has warned us that the human heart is deceitful and beyond cure.[8] Many people have pronounced the famous last words, 'It could never happen to me.'

   One morning a pastor rang me and asked if he could come for counsel. As he put his foot across the threshold he burst into tears. 'I didn't think it could happen to me,' he cried. But it had, just because he had failed to recognise the strength of his sexuality and the depravity of the human heart. We need to take special care when we are under stress, weakened with illness, tired or lonely. These conditions can make us very vulnerable to temptation.

4. Fourthly we must be careful not to lie to ourselves. It is very easy to deceive ourselves about the reality and consequences of our actions. How many people have crossed the situational boundaries which surrounded their workplace or church activities and when questioned have excused it with, 'Yes, but it's only platonic.' John Powell considers that from adolescence onwards there is no such thing as a 'purely platonic' relationship. Sex will be a strong element whether it is subconscious or consciously acknowledged.[9]

   Others have foolishly crossed the proper boundaries and have then convinced themselves it must be all right because 'it feels so good'. Another incredible excuse I have heard is: 'If it isn't right, why doesn't God stop us?' As if God ever treats us as puppets.

For Consideration:
Make a list of relationships both at work and outside.
Place a mark beside the name of anyone to whom you
are attracted.
Are you free to pursue the relationship further?
Is he or she free to become a close friend?
Are you in any danger of crossing a situational or
emotional boundary because it seems good and desirable?
Have you already stepped over a God-placed boundary
with someone, either situationally or emotionally?

Putting things right
Inevitably there will be people who despite clear warnings
will cross the boundaries. You may be one of these. If so
what should you do?

1. The first step is to recognise and admit that a boundary
   has been crossed, or is in danger of being crossed. The
   prodigal son's first step back to his father was when he
   came to his senses and recognised the plight he was in.[10]

2. The next step will be to turn back. If you have
   overstepped the limit then the right thing is to step back
   across the boundary. One of Evan Hopkins' children
   once asked his father what he should do when he had
   sinned. Evan Hopkins drew a circle with many doors
   and told him that if he had left the circle through a
   certain door, then the way back was through the same
   door. If he had come out through the door marked
   'anger', being angry with his sister, for example, then
   the way back was to repent of that anger with his sister
   and to say sorry. Repentance is simply to turn around
   and go in the opposite direction.

3. At this point a very helpful and biblical step would
   be to find a mature Christian before whom you could
   make a full confession and from whom you could
   receive some spiritual direction.[11]

4. Be prepared to take the consequences of your sin and work at putting things right where possible.

5. Lastly you may need to seek help to resolve any past hurts which could be weakening your resistance to temptation.

The blockages, the hindrances and the traps experienced in relationships are likely to be caused by buried hurts and unmet emotional needs. Although no one should be encouraged to avoid responsibility for his sin, until these emotional problems are addressed and healing sought, one could easily continue to be entangled by such snares.

HEALING THE WOUNDED CHILD

As we have seen the child of a dysfunctional family system frequently grows up to become a dysfunctional adult who struggles with difficult problems. His painful childhood may have caused him to form many false assumptions about life and to contend with painful feelings which surface at inconvenient moments. These irrational beliefs and unhealed pain will affect the way he approaches relationships or once involved, the way he behaves within them. The behaviour is often unhealthy and serves to endorse the misconceptions and only momentarily to dull the pain.

This correlation between a man's thoughts, emotions and behaviour can be seen in Scripture. God says, 'I the Lord search the *heart* and examine the *mind* to reward a man according to his *conduct* according to what his *deeds* deserve.'[1] The psalmist also makes the same connection. 'Search me, O God, and know my *heart*; test me and know my anxious *thoughts*. See if there is any offensive *way* in me, and lead me in the way everlasting.'[2] [Italics mine.]

Every dysfunctional adult will need to work at these three areas before he or she is able to fully enjoy stable and satisfying friendships. Until this work is done the misconceptions, the painful feelings and the resulting behaviour patterns will continue to trouble and upset every new relationship.

You may have identified with the difficulties of either making or keeping relationships or you may have fallen into one of the traps mentioned. Your present relationship difficulty could be just the tip of the iceberg. The tip is the part that can be seen and identified. In fact it is only a small part of the whole. The rest is submerged and goes unrecognised. While only the tip of the problem is examined there will be no lasting resolution. The whole thing must be brought out into the open and each part appropriately dealt with.

Jesus said, 'Then you will know the truth and the truth will set you free.'[3] If this is so, why do so many Christians read or hear the truth daily and yet continue to hold misconceptions about different aspects of life? It would seem that in many instances the truth has had only a superficial penetration. Hidden within each of us is the child we once were. Certainly all the experiences of our childhood have been recorded together with our reactions to them. It is this inner part of us that needs to hear the truth. So often I meet people who have been Christians for twenty years or more who are still reacting to the sort of misconceptions and painful feelings we have mentioned in previous chapters. Usually when given the opportunity to talk about their problems they will inadvertently refer to a hidden part of themselves, usually a part they despise.

A lady sat in my office a short while ago and told me about the childish way she reacted in certain situations. Not only was she puzzled by it but it also created a difficulty in her relationships. When I asked her to describe a recent experience along with the feelings and thoughts which the experience had prompted, she struggled to do so. She obviously felt very ashamed of her behaviour. At one point she hung her head for a moment and said, 'It's such a tacky part of me.' Several times in the conversation she referred to this 'tacky' part of herself with embarrassment.

Another person described having 'a bit inside that's bad'. Whilst yet another referred to, 'the stupid bit of myself'. One young man called it, 'the weak part of me'. This phenomenon of a 'hidden self' is extremely common. I refer to it in my book, *A Healing Fellowship:*

It is amazing how many people enter counselling and admit to feeling either as though they were two personalities or of having an unknown part of themselves hidden away. It is a part they are afraid of. It is full of bad feelings. They feel it should be kept out of sight. Frequently the picture that comes into their minds as we pray is of a child locked in a cave or cupboard; an unacceptable child; a bad child, who is impossible to love.[4]

It may be that during childhood these people were fed lies about themselves. Or perhaps painful experiences caused them to draw wrong conclusions. These thoughts provoked such bad feelings that the child began to hide what she considered to be the evil, unacceptable, shameful part and only to show the acceptable part. Gradually this became a way of life for her and the child with the bad feelings was buried, not dead but alive. In time an 'adapted adult' emerges who has conveniently forgotten about the hidden child. Only now and again there is a baffling childish reaction which the adult quickly suppresses with condemning words, such as, 'That's disgusting,' 'Don't be such a weakling,' or, 'That's so tacky.' But hitting the child on the head in this way does not exterminate her, nor does it heal her. Until the child within each of us is given recognition, is brought to Jesus for healing and hears the truth from God, there will be no real change – just superficial modifications. The good news has to penetrate beyond the adapted adult of the present into the child of the past.

I may not like to admit it, 'But I am the child that was.'[5] I may outwardly be a knowledgeable, mature adult dressed in sophisticated clothes. But inside I am, in many respects, still that child. In *Pursuing Sexual Wholeness* by Andy Comiskey, a man describes his childhood molestation; his growing feelings of being unacceptable to his family and peers and the consequent construction of a socially acceptable self behind which to hide a frightened child. He says that on becoming a Christian his false front was still strong and safe. But inside the pretty package he had made was a five-year-old little boy curled up in the corner of a dark empty room, beaten and hurt. He writes:

> Through various relationships and events, the Lord began to tear down the walls I had built up to imprison the ugly child one brick at a time . . . Jesus is still at work, and the construction signs are still up. And if you listen very carefully, you can still hear the sounds of a jackhammer. But when you look again, you will see a young boy growing up in the loving arms of his heavenly Father. He is no longer afraid and alone. So next time you meet a cold, angry person who is hard to like, look again and you might see a young child alone and afraid in a dark room, terrified to let anyone in to love him. And if you listen very closely, you may hear him crying out for someone to save him from his emptiness.[6]

One of the reasons we try so hard to banish and destroy that obnoxious, childish, stupid, inconsistent, vulnerable, needy part of ourselves, is because we usually view it as shamefully sinful. We try repenting of it and dying to it, but the wounded child needs healing not killing. The stockpile of angry thoughts, the bitterness and self-indulgent behaviour are the things which need to be repented of. They spoil our relationships with one another and with our Heavenly Father and need to receive a death blow, not the hurting inner-self. That part needs healing and Jesus was anointed to heal the brokenhearted and bind up their wounds.[7]

Frightened and unhappy children find ways of coping with their difficult circumstances. Although they may choose an unhealthy way, it is understandable and excusable given their situation. However, when these same devices are carried forward and used by adults they can be viewed as unnecessary and ungodly.

A child who shuts down the need to be held and cuddled because it was too painful to have the need unmet is coping in the only way he knows. Years later when the adult rejects a loving touch from a friend or spouse it may be understandable, but it is certainly an inappropriate reaction and is one which could be viewed as ungodly in a Christian.

Another child may suffer a similar experience of insufficient physical contact which in turn would create the same intense hunger to be held and fondled. Instead of shut-down this child may retain those feelings. However, this does not give him permission as an adult to indulge in sexual promiscuity in order to appease his hunger for physical contact. In other words, though our inner child needs to be recognised he should not be allowed to dictate present behaviour.

The question we must ask ourselves is, how can this wounded child of the past be healed and freed to mature and integrate with the adult part?

Each of the following steps in the process of healing is important, but not the order in which they are tackled. As a person opens up his life to the Holy Spirit He leads him on his own unique and individual journey to wholeness. The pattern I have set out is the one most commonly followed, though frequently a person will set out on the journey and pass with apparent ease through the first two stages and then stop. He may then feel the first stage was incomplete and so he regresses for a while, or he may find a particular part of the process extremely hard and will need to take his time at that point. After each step some work has been suggested and prayers outlined. These are for those who are anxious to take every opportunity to open themselves to God's healing.

Steps to Healing the Wounded Child
The first step is always the same.

1. Owning the Problem
Before any healing can be received or any changes made, we must admit to having a problem and we must acknowledge it as ours. It is always less painful to apportion the blame to someone else, or to see oneself simply as a victim of circumstances, or somebody's stupidity. It is true that

others may have had a major role in creating the problem or are compounding the present difficulties, but by focusing on these issues we forever avoid facing the reality of our painful feelings, irrational beliefs and resulting behaviour. It takes courage to face up to the results of our self-centred search for satisfaction and happiness. To ignore the difficulties we have in making or keeping relationships, or to minimise the seriousness of the unhealthy and unwise relationships we have made, is to prefer darkness rather than light. This is a non-healing route.

Work: In a notebook or personal journal, write a full description of your present problem.

Prayer: Heavenly Father this is my problem ... (read your problem aloud to God). Because it is my problem it is therefore my responsibility to work at finding the underlying causes for it and then to seek healing and a solution to it. Father, I ask for the help of your Holy Spirit in this work. In Jesus' name. Amen.

Once the problem is owned the work of healing can begin.

2. Owning the Child

The concept of an 'inner child' may be too difficult or unpalatable for some. It is certainly not vital for healing that this idea should be adopted. The only reason for referring to an 'inner child' is because the term connects the adult of the present who has problems, with the child of the past who was hurt. The child's rational and emotional reaction to the hurt inevitably led on to the present difficulties. The term 'inner child' also gives an impression of immaturity. It is certainly true that many adults struggle with immature reactions. Ninety-nine per cent of the time a person will react in a mature and reasonable manner but suddenly something touches a 'hot button' and he is spun into making an immature and childish response. It is as if one area of life has never properly grown up and such a person needs to reconnect with that part in order for it to be healed and released to mature.

I encountered an example of this at a recent conference. A young lawyer told me about his problem with homosexuality. He seemed physically and mentally well-developed and he had been a Christian for several years, so was presumably growing spiritually. Only his sexual development seemed to have been arrested. There were several reasons for this. Mostly the cause lay in an over-identification with a very possessive mother. But he had also lacked a father figure and had received little affirmation of his masculinity. The journey to wholeness for this young man would be to reconnect with the arrested part of himself and take the steps necessary for growth to occur. The 'little boy' would need to separate emotionally from his mother and the 'teenager' would need his masculinity affirmed. His present reactions will not change until these vital steps have been taken. Although the proper time for taking these steps has long passed for this young man, with God all things are possible. God can enable him to connect significantly with the past and enable him to complete the unfinished business of his childhood.

This step of reconnecting with the place of arrested growth does not need to be very dramatic. It may be just an acknowledgment of an immature response in certain situations.

Alex wanted help to sort out some very childish reactions she experienced with close friends. As she chatted about her childhood she made a passing comment about her father never wanting her to grow up. As we prayed together she went back to the little girl who wanted to please her father by staying immature. It was an unemotional connection with the 'little girl of the past'. Before God she renounced her desire to be what her father wanted and instead accepted God's purpose for her life, which was to grow up and become mature.

My first personal experience of this took place before we had very much understanding of inner healing. I was

praying with a friend and had asked God to show me
why I often suffered from anxiety for no apparent reason.
Almost immediately I had a picture of a three-year-old child
sitting in the corner of a cage looking decidedly miserable.
I recognised the child as being myself. I viewed her from
a distance, not liking what I saw. I was slightly chastened
when I realised that Jesus was there and not rejecting her,
as I was. Several times in prayer I had a similar experience
and each time I felt unable to accept the child.

During this period I had several dreams about children;
one was particularly significant. I dreamed I was getting
married and had two little bridesmaids in attendance. One
of the two was ready, waiting and looking very sweet.
The other was not yet dressed. She looked grubby and
forlorn. I felt angry and looked around for someone to
get the child ready immediately. Everyone was busy and
it began to dawn on me that I was the only one available
and that in fact it was my wedding and therefore my
responsibility to take the child in hand. This dream was
a turning point for me. For the first time I owned and took
responsibility for my own 'inner child'.

This incident illustrates an important truth. God 'reveals
deep and hidden things; he knows what lies in darkness,
and light dwells with him'.[8] We may not understand our
reactions; they may appear to have no connection with
the past. With my rational mind I could not link my
anxiety with my childhood. The past may be submerged
and hidden from the conscious mind, but it is not concealed
from God and He is able to reveal it to us through dreams
and visions. 'For God does speak – now one way, now
another – though man may not perceive it. In a dream,
in a vision of the night when deep sleep falls on men
as they slumber in their beds.'[9]

How we view this immature part of ourselves is not
important. It is only essential that we acknowledge the
painful memories and buried feelings which belong to our
childhood. We must make the connection in the same way
as the seventy-five-year-old man had to connect up with
the feelings of the five-year-old whose mother had died.

∗

Prayer: Heavenly Father I need your help to reconnect with my childhood. As I do this work I pray that you will bring back to my memory those unresolved issues which are important for me to remember. I know that I have suppressed many incidents with the feelings and I give you permission to bring them back to consciousness. I give you the control of those memories and ask that this work be done in your time. I ask this in the name of Jesus who specialises in binding up broken hearts. Amen.

Work: 1. In your journal write a description of your childhood home. Not just how it looked but also how it felt to you.

2. Write a letter first to your mother and then to your father (not to be sent). Tell them how you felt about the relationship you had with them when you were a child; what you enjoyed, what you disliked and what you missed. Tell them how you felt about their relationship with each other.

3. Write a similar letter to anyone else who was in any way important in your childhood.

4. Write a description of any childhood incident which comes to mind and generates difficult feelings.

Prayer: Heavenly Father as far as I am able I want to own the child I once was. This is how I see him (or her) now in my memory . . . I know that parts of me are not fully mature and I want to reconnect with those parts so that I can take any steps necessary to grow up. I ask you to help me not to bury the child again, but to recognise him (or her) and take responsibility for that bit of myself. In Jesus' name. Amen.

Making this connection is an important part of the healing process. And so too is the next step.

3. Mourning Childhood Losses
A lonely child who grew up in isolation from other children, missed the joy and fun of relationships. A little girl who

was continually molested sexually by her father lost the innocence and trust which rightfully belonged to her. The boy who was never encouraged or praised by his father missed the joy of being valued by one of the most important people in his life. Bereavement or loss in whatever form it comes, is not resolved until it has been properly grieved over.

The seventy-five-year-old man who lost his mother at the age of five needed to mourn the loss of love, security and nurture that her death had caused him. The seven-year-old who lived through perpetual criticism needs to grieve the loss of acceptance. The isolated child must grieve the loss of fun. The child who looked after a sick parent must grieve the loss of freedom from adult responsibility. For all these children there has been significant deprivation. Parts of their childhood have been lost and this needs to be properly mourned before healing can take place.

Work: The working-out process is best done with another person. Strong feelings may surface and it is safer if someone else is there. Choose a mature Christian person who can handle grief.

First give yourself permission to grieve your losses fully. When you have done this ask God to help you.

Then, aloud, tell God about the things you have missed out on or lost when you were a child. Tell Him the feelings that accompanied these deprivations and as you do so express those feelings in whatever way you can.

Remember this work has to be your own. You are the only one who can do your grief work. No one else can do it for you.

Dangers: When the sad experiences of the past are looked at, instead of cleansing grief and closure of the wound, a person may occasionally fall into the trap of self-pity. Such a route leads nowhere and usually occurs because of a yearning for comfort and sympathy.

*

Tips: Connecting with the feelings is difficult for some people. It may help to visualise your mother or your father in front of you and then tell them aloud how you felt about your childhood. Tell them what it felt like to be abandoned, picked on, sexually molested, beaten, criticised, or whatever it was. As you do this allow the feelings to surface and do not swallow them down again.

Grieving takes time and there is no hurrying this part of the process. It may come out in fits and starts and be mixed with the next vital step of forgiveness.

4. Forgiveness

As the grief begins and the pain is expressed, anger towards the perpetrators of the hurt may also begin to surface and this needs to be acknowledged. Some people express their anger very forcefully but others seem to be relieved with only a verbal admission of anger. Once the feelings of loss and anger are out in the open a person is ready to begin the process of forgiving. It is rarely accomplished in a one-off prayer. In most cases it needs to be repeated several times before the ardent desire for justice and punishment can be laid down and the incident can be remembered without pain.

I remember praying for an incest victim who connected feelingly with the tormented five-year-old, many, many times. Usually forgiveness was expressed in between feelings of pain and anger. The release of pain, anger and forgiveness came to an end almost simultaneously.

Because forgiveness is such an important issue for a Christian we are warned by psychologists, Drs Hemfelt, Minirth and Meier, to beware of forgiving without emotional integrity.[10] This can happen when a Christian comes out of denial, sees the past as it really was, acknowledges the hurts that were incurred and then moves straight into forgiveness. Jesus talked about forgiving from the heart.[11] Until we have connected with the feelings of the wounded child and have begun to express them, forgiveness will only be from the rational mind. We are doing it because it is right to do so. It is true that we cannot always wait for the right feelings before we do what is correct, but when forgiveness is done in this way the temptation is to shut the door too quickly and think that the healing process is over. Sometimes there is more intregrity in telling God that you need His help to forgive because at the moment it is too difficult. The key is always in expressing the difficult feelings. Once the poison is out of the infected wound, cleansing and healing come naturally.

Work: Make a list of the major hurts in your life. Beside the hurt write the name of the person who inflicted it.

In prayer forgive the person for that specific hurt and when you have done so cross the hurt off the list and the person's name. When this has been done destroy the list.

Prayer: Heavenly Father I know I have to forgive but I can only do this work with your help. I ask that you help me continue to release the bad feelings so that I can truly forgive from the heart. Now, Father, I forgive . . . for the hurt he (or she) caused me when . . . (repeat this until every incident is dealt with). I do this in the name of Jesus.

Father, I ask that you will forgive me for the bitterness and resentment I have harboured all these years. I now lay down my desire to punish these people and I hand them over to you. Help me Father to bless them from now on. In Jesus' name. Amen.

5. Healing

Making a connection with the child of the past uncovers the painful wounds so that God can penetrate with His healing. Most childhood hurts were caused through abusive, neglectful or careless parenting. None of us can return physically to our childhood and make up what we missed. Whether it was a loss of nurture, encouragement, affirmation, or a failure to separate from mother, or to become fully autonomous and self-reliant, or to come to a place of self-acceptance, it is impossible ever to recover the loss in the natural. Nor can another person in the present make it up to us, however much we may long for them to do so. Only God can reach into our innermost being and heal the wounds and make up the deficit. There can be no substitute for God.

This part of the work must not be hurried. God will do it in His time and in His way. Jesus promised that those who mourn will be comforted.[12] He may bring this comfort through a dream, a vision, a picture, a word of Scripture, a sense of His presence, or He may combine several of these to heal us.

Prayer: Heavenly Father as far as I am able I have emptied out all the grief within my wounded heart. I have forgiven those who were careless, or cruel, or just did not understand or listen to me. And now I ask you to come and heal me. I know that no one except you Father, can make up to me what I have lost during my childhood. Please fulfil your promise and send your Holy Spirit to comfort me. I commit myself to seek only your face for healing and am prepared to wait until you do it. Amen.

Work: Spend time seeking God's face. Especially at night make this petition before you fall asleep.

Avoid your usual means of comforting yourself. (Such as – fantasising, eating, reading, television, etc. Not because all these things are wrong, but because when used to avoid discomfort they prop us up and prevent God breaking into our brokenness.)

6. Renouncing the False Assumptions

Jesus was anointed to 'bind up the broken hearted' and so far the process has been directed at healing the wounds. But Jesus also came to 'proclaim freedom for the captives and release for the prisoners'.[13] The false assumptions made and stored by a hurt child can be very binding and an important step in the total healing process is the uncovering of these misconceptions and renouncing them.

A young man confessed that he was plagued by perfectionism. He lived on a roller-coaster of anxiety and depression. He would set himself impossible goals which only served to make him very anxious in case he failed to reach them. Then when the inevitable happened and he failed, he would sink back again into depression and self-hatred. The root of his problem lay in his inability ever to please his highly critical father. As a small boy his goal in life had been to win an approving nod from his dad. His self-worth depended on it. Before he could begin on the road to freedom he had to renounce his irrational belief that his true worth was still dependent on men's approval.

Many relationship problems are rooted in unrealistic expectations and misconceptions, probably formed as a result of past experiences. Healing the past bad experiences alone will not remove the problem. The expectations and beliefs must also be uncovered, renounced as irrational and replaced with healthy ones.

Prayer: Heavenly Father I ask you to help me to be really honest with myself. Please show me if I am holding on to any misconceptions about life, about myself, about relationships and especially about you. Show me too Father, if I am setting myself any unrealistic goals in my life, or if I have wrong expectations of others. In Jesus' name. Amen.

Work: Make a list of any misconceptions, unrealistic goals and unrealistic expectations that you have become aware of as you have read the previous chapters.

7. Renewal of the Mind

Once a belief is renounced a vacuum is left. If John Smith has spent his entire life with the co-dependent belief that he is responsible for making other people happy, when he renounces that belief what is he left with? A void. Even a loss of identity. Renewing the mind is the process whereby irrational beliefs, unreasonable expectations and mistaken goals are replaced with biblical concepts, realistic hopes and godly aims.

At this point in the process time spent building a relationship with God is invaluable. The truth has to be sought and received at gut level. Healing releases a person to receive the truth. This now has an opportunity to penetrate the whole personality and to free the person at the depths of his being.

As the truth begins to penetrate changes begin to happen from the inside out. Unnoticed and imperceptibly the old passes away and all things become new.[14] The only thing that will prevent this process is a lack of willingness for it to continue. Many years ago a lady called Vicky sought help for depression. Over a period of several years God healed her quite significantly. Her depression lifted and she was able to take up activities which had fallen by the wayside. At this point she stopped. She decided she had had as much change as she could cope with. In several areas she still lacked freedom and in many respects lives a limited life today. But God will not take away her free-will. If she opens her life to the process of change once again God will recommence the work He began within her.

Work: Using the list you have already made work through each item and ask God to show you a godly belief, goal or expectation to correct the one on your list.

When you are stuck spend time praying and asking God to speak to you.

When you read the Bible underline verses which counter your misconceptions.

8. Changing Behaviour
Behaviour is the visible part of our lives. It is driven by the hidden feelings and beliefs we hold. These two are like the power or the fuel that keeps a vehicle on the road. Once the fuel has run out the vehicle loses its power to run. However, we cannot always wait until we have fully dealt with the hurts and the misconceptions before we change

our behaviour. Often our unhealthy behaviour is creating difficulties and problems in our relationships and we need to start changing it immediately, even before the healing has started. It may actually be downright sinful behaviour and so it has to be stopped quickly. We cannot use unhealed hurt as an excuse for maintaining ungodly behaviour.

The parish priest who becomes sexually involved with his lady deacon has to recognise his behaviour as sinful and repent of it before anything else happens. After this he may seek a spiritual director or counsellor who can help him towards the necessary healing.

Another reason we may need, early in the process, to drop or change some of our habits, is because these practices often feed and maintain our problem.

For instance Caroline loves to fantasise. She imagines very happy scenes where she does everything perfectly and her friends think she is wonderful. The problem arises when a few days later she meets up with a group of friends and nothing goes as she imagined. She disagrees with one of them. She disappoints another. Her dreams are dashed and she is disillusioned with friendship. Her fantasies not only maintain her relationship problems by creating unreal expectations, but also serve as an escape from inner pain which must be faced before God can heal it.

In the same way a homosexual must deal early with his fantasy life. His problem is often fed and maintained by his thoughts. Before dropping off to sleep people with homosexual tendencies, male or female, will usually comfort themselves with fantasies of being touched and held by their idol. This is often accompanied by masturbation. The thoughts in conjunction with the actions keep the sexual neurosis fed and no healing will take place until this is given up.

Some behaviour does not appear to be particularly harmful or sinful and often we fail to recognise the manipulative, deceptive aspects of it. It may be quite far on in the healing process that truth dawns and we see our conduct as ungodly as well as unhealthy. At this point we must confess our sins before God. As we have already said elsewhere, it is biblical and certainly helpful to make this confession before a mature Christian who could then pronounce forgiveness according to 1 John 1:9.

Repentance involves not only turning from the old behaviour but the struggle to find a new and more Christ-like way of conducting our lives.

Work: Make a list of the ungodly and unhealthy behaviour patterns which have been operating in your life. Especially those which have caused or added to your relationship problems.

Prayer: Heavenly Father, I repent of my ungodly behaviour. I ask you to forgive me for . . . (confess aloud either to God alone, or with a mature friend, those things you have listed). Father, I ask you to send your Holy Spirit to help me and give me the strength to turn from these practices. Show me the way to behave, especially with my friends and give me a nudge whenever I slip back into the old patterns. Father, I want to be more like Jesus. Please transform me day by day. Amen.

Work: Read 1 John 1:9 aloud.

Spend time now just receiving His forgiveness.

Use the old list of ungodly behaviour patterns to make a new list of new patterns. Each old one needs a new one to replace it.

For example:

Old Behaviour	*New Behaviour*
Using silence manipulatively	Talk about my feelings
Fantasising before I fall asleep	Listen to a music tape
	Read the Bible

Once healing is taking place we are ready to look at friendship from a new and positive perspective.

THE WORK OF FRIENDSHIP

As already suggested the foundations for a good friendship are love, sharing, trust and commitment. To build on less would be to erect a shaky edifice in danger of imminent collapse. When these four elements are in place between people, we have the basic requirements necessary for that good friendship.

As each of these vital elements are developed in their various ways a friendship should become a rich and vibrant relationship. The growth of the friendship is directly connected to the amount of work each person is prepared to invest in it. 'Love works for those who work at it.'[1] So let's consider how we develop love.

Love

Love should be the primary requirement for any friendship. One of the last instructions Jesus gave to the men he called his friends was 'love one another'. Saint Paul wrote an amazing description of this quality to the Church in Corinth (which we have already cited in chapter 2).[2] How can we love like that?

With Forgiveness

'Love keeps no record of wrongs.'[3] Unless forgiveness is practised from the beginning, the relationship will never be more than a 'flash in the pan' or a good idea which never quite gets off the ground. At first a new friend is an unknown quantity, which is exciting and challenging but this lack of familiarity can also make one prone to making mistakes.

The person responsible for putting right the hurt or mistake is the one who made it – the offender. The moment one becomes aware of causing offence to one's friend one should be prepared to make that simple request: 'Will you forgive me?' This is 'the magic enabler and facilitator of dialogue'. John Powell reckons that most ailing relationships can be restored to health almost miraculously by this simple but sincere request.[4]

It can feel humiliating to acknowledge a blunder and ask for forgiveness but the humiliation is due only to the mistaken idea that to be wrong is to be devalued in the other person's eyes. Actually it is usually quite the opposite. Providing the other person really does love you and wants to forgive, he feels only respect and gratitude. He knows that it is never easy to eat humble pie. The reward makes it worth the effort; a restored relationship at a greater level of intimacy.

But it could happen that the person who has caused the hurt is quite unaware of the pain which he has inflicted. When this happens how can the friendship be restored? The key is in communication – an open and honest sharing of feelings by the one who is hurt. In many relationships this may be impossible to achieve. For example it may not be right to share the hurts of one's childhood with a reserved and elderly parent. In such a situation the pain can only be shared with God and perhaps a mature friend. Friendship, however, is different. It would be disloyal to share the hurt first with another person before talking it over with the 'offending' friend. Of course one shares the problem with God, but only with permission from, or together with, the friend should it be shared with another person.

So the right step is to acknowledge the hurt to one's friend. It is no good feeling hurt and resentful, but saying nothing. Nor is it any good feeling hurt and pretending nothing is wrong. If the friend has no idea that what he said or did was hurtful how can he say sorry and put it right? How can he avoid repeating the same thing again if he doesn't know it to be wrong? Careless actions or words are more easily overlooked with acquaintances but with an ongoing friendship they cannot afford to be glossed over.

I am rather a stickler for punctuality. Lateness really offends me. Lack of punctuality in acquaintances is not so important to me but in my friendships it matters. When I am trying to relate on an almost daily basis with someone who is frequently late then I need to acknowledge my feelings about this to the person concerned. This is not in order to apportion blame but only to be open about one's feelings. Any hidden agenda is like dry rot in a relationship. It will eventually ruin the friendship.

As soon as the hurt has been acknowledged by the one hurt, it is over to the friend either to explain his behaviour or to own the offence and ask for forgiveness. If this does not happen it is stalemate. David and I went out to supper a short while ago with some close friends. I assumed it was to be a relaxed evening around the fire and so I had not changed. David was not comfortable with this and thought I should wear something smarter. I had left it rather late to change so stayed as I was. On arrival we discovered the evening to be more formal than I had anticipated and I could tell that David was put out. When one's partner is proved right it is never easy and the temptation is to ignore it, to gloss over it or worse still, to find an accusing retort. 'Well *you* didn't wear the right thing last week.' Obviously the way to a resolution is to own the fault. 'If you are willing to admit you are all wrong when you are all wrong, you are all right.'[5] The other options lead to resentment, loss of respect and loss of intimacy.

Once the responsibility for inflicting pain has been owned and the simple request for forgiveness has been made, the last step before full restoration can take place is for the offended partner to release forgiveness to the offender.

Josh McDowell says that: 'Forgiveness is the oil of relationships.' An unforgiving person can never develop a truly intimate and lasting relationship. Though a person be intelligent and skilled he can never have an intimate relationship – it would be torn apart by a stockpile of unforgotten conflicts which remain unforgiven.[6]

Two friends may be Christians and may be well versed in the importance of forgiveness, but this will not make forgiveness any easier. It is hard to forgive, but it is excruciating to feel unforgiven.

What does forgiveness really mean? A dictionary definition puts it this way: 'To pardon, or cease to feel resentment against (a person): to pardon, overlook (a debt or trespass). To be merciful or forgiving.'[7] True forgiveness is costly, especially when it means overlooking the offence and reinstating the person as if he had never caused hurt. Human beings are naturally self-protective. It is built into their make-up. Therefore to reinstate a friend who has carelessly let one down would be to make oneself vulnerable to being hurt again. Besides it just isn't fair! If one has suffered through someone else's carelessness why should the other person get off scot-free? Justice calls for punishment and one of the ways we punish is to withhold forgiveness. As well as a desire for justice and self-protection our 'inner teacher' or 'critical parent' tells us that our friend will never learn a lesson if we let him off the hook too quickly.

When struggling to release forgiveness it is helpful to remember that we may also need to be forgiven at some point in the relationship. 'When I refuse to forgive, I am burning a bridge that someday I will need to pass over.'[8]

To forgive one needs a certain largeness of heart. I once deeply offended a friend by something I said. She wrote and told me how hurt she was. When I received the letter I felt quite devastated that I had been so careless and immediately wrote back owning the fault and asking her to forgive me. On receiving my apology she

immediately and freely forgave me and I remember feeling
immensely grateful for such generosity.

With Generosity

Generosity is an important aspect of love and some people
find it easier than others. It would seem that children
who have been conditionally loved find it hard to love
generously as adults. It is as if their store of love is scarce
and they tend not to want to give too much away. They
give of themselves meanly and receive from others with
equal measure, though others may be giving to them very
bountifully. It takes generosity both to give and to receive.
It is so discouraging and unrewarding to give a hug and to
find oneself hugging a rigid frame, or to give a compliment
and have it dropped in the dustbin as if it were valueless.
To refuse or throw away a present from a friend would be
extremely rude and few would ever do that, but many refuse
the everyday gifts of love from their friends. They shrug them
off with: 'Oh, I'm not much good at that sort of thing.' And
one may not be particularly good at it, for various reasons.
However, if one wishes for a lasting friendship one will have
to learn the art of receiving generously.

I have struggled for many years with a tendency to
be slightly aloof. I would more naturally shake hands
than kiss a person and I forget that others were brought
up to enjoy and expect much warmer expressions of
love. Though my husband and other friends have been
good at reminding me, the greatest help I received was
being meted out some of my own medicine. I had been
co-counselling with a person I knew fairly well and at the
end of our session we said goodbye to our counsellee and
I settled back in my chair to debrief with my counselling
partner. To my surprise she simply mumbled good night
and left. I remained in my chair for some time feeling
slightly dazed. I sensed that the evening had not been
appropriately terminated and that I had somehow been
devalued. I took note of the experience and decided
that if I wanted to keep my friends I must work at

becoming more generous in my expressions of affection and appreciation.

With Kindness

Another aspect of love is kindness. Because it is usually understood to be a natural ingredient in every friendship it is rarely considered necessary to mention it. Sadly the milk of human kindness does not go far in the face of failed expectations and dashed hopes. These disappointments can turn potential friends into cruel enemies. I have watched several friendships that started as very healing relationships deteriorate into hurtful battlegrounds. Unfortunately the openness and sharing that had been present in the initial stages of the friendship will have provided inside information that can so easily be used as destructive ammunition.

The best precaution one can take is prayer. Friendship of the sort we are discussing is for gentle people whose hurts have not caused them to build brittle structures around themselves. The clever, quick, thrusting person is often very attractive and as a casual friend may be very stimulating and amusing company. However, this sort of person often lacks the gentleness and kindness necessary for a loving and lasting friendship. So one should pray for wisdom in choosing a friend. One needs to ask oneself if this friend is likely to respect the shared confidences and not pass them on to others nor use them destructively at a later date.

Once a friendship is initiated prayer is needed for sensitivity, that both partners will be 'clothed with compassion, kindness, gentleness and patience', that truly both will be able to 'Bear with each other and forgive whatever grievances you may have against one another.'9

For Consideration:

How quickly do you forgive your friend when he or she hurts you?

When you are in the wrong do you:

– gloss over it?
– blame shift?
– attack back with an accusing retort?
– own up and ask for forgiveness?
Are you generous at giving love to your friends?
Are you generous at receiving their love?
When your friend has disappointed you what has been your reaction?

Sharing
A relationship usually starts when two people meet and some common interest encourages them to pursue the relationship further. They begin by sharing information and providing both are free for it, this may be the beginnings of a lasting friendship.

Past History
Friendship is two-way. It begins with a journey of discovery for both. To know your new friend's history is not just interesting, it is invaluable to your understanding of him. When I first met David and learned that he was the ninth child of a family of ten, I had immediate insight into his competitiveness and his incredible ability to devour lunch in five minutes flat. With so many older brothers and sisters a small boy had very little chance of getting a second helping unless he ate in double-quick time! In the case of another friend I was slightly baffled by her un-British way of drawing close to people in a very short time. The mystery was solved when I learned she was a twin.

Time spent with a new friend hearing about his or her past and sharing one's own is never wasted. In fact it is indispensable for the building of a friendship. Frequently the past can only be explored through family anecdotes and photos but occasionally it is possible to spend a day exploring the childhood haunts of a friend. To see the church pew where David had naughtily scratched his name when a small boy and the rectory pond where he floated a home-made raft, made me feel a part of his childhood. With another friend I spent a day visiting her old school. I saw the dormitory where she had slept and the dining room where she had eaten her meals. Sharing the past in this way provides a good springboard for friendship.

Communication

Sharing is a fundamental aspect of friendship and is achieved by various means. The most obvious being communication.

Just as the past is explained and explored mainly through words so the relationship will be developed mostly through conversation. This may sound very obvious and yet many of us are more adept at 'keeping ourselves to ourselves' than sharing ourselves. There are three necessary ingredients to communication: talking, listening and understanding.[10] It is possible to talk and give important information to one's friend only to discover it has not been heard. Frequently I have had a now familiar experience when ready for sleep with my husband. In the quiet closeness of snuggling up in bed I have shared some important bit of news only to realise that David has not been listening at all. Silence, interrupted by heavy breathing, tells me he is already fast asleep!

Sharing through communication has to be a two-way occupation. Whilst one talks the other must listen. To talk to someone who is not listening leaves one feeling uninteresting and valueless. The proof that one has really been heard comes when the listener gives a response which shows he has understood.

I learned early in life to be a good listener. My older sisters were in their late teens when I was still a child. They often needed a listening ear and little sisters are renowned for their fascination with the romances of their elders. I never missed a word. My rapt attention and frequent gasps always assured them that they had been well and truly heard. Later I would show the full extent of my understanding, though not to them. At school, after lights-out, I would recount highly embellished accounts of my sisters' amorous activities. Then it was my turn to be listened to with rapt attention!

At the beginning of a relationship these three ingredients are indispensable. A short while ago two friends shared with me some difficulties they were experiencing in their relatively new friendship. It was obvious that though they had talked and listened they had fallen short in understanding. When I asked what were their expectations of the relationship they both said: 'friendship'. But simply sharing that expectation with each other was not enough. They needed to go one step further and understand what each had meant by that. In fact we discovered together that they both held very different views about friendship and what it entailed. Early in any relationship expectations should be discussed until a mutually satisfying agreement about them is reached.

Misunderstanding and mistakes are easily made unless time is spent communicating on important issues. Friends are not necessarily good mind-readers. A common but doomed-to-fail expectation is that a friend should intuit one's mood and then do or say the right thing. It does occasionally happen but more often it does not and then disappointment follows, with anger and blame in tow. In an adult relationship both parties will openly discuss their hopes for their friendship. In this way they eventually come to a mutual understanding of what is reasonable to expect. Even in an adult relationship childish communication is often more in evidence than mature sharing, but it is these childish and manipulative practices of silence, withdrawal, pouting, whining and blaming which spoil so many potential friendships.

Minor irritations and differences are more easily suppressed, ignored, or communicated inadequately. A frank discussion may be painful but unless differences are shared they quickly grow into major difficulties. And it is not necessary to raise one's voice to be frank! Understanding, appreciation and compromise can be arrived at once they are discussed. The mark of a mature friendship is the ability of both parties to make tolerable compromises.

Encouragement

I am married to an encourager *par excellence* (I would not be writing this book if not), so I have first-hand experience of the enriching and positive effect of this type of communication. Sincere encouragement is a generous act of love. One highlights not one's own strength and ability, but those belonging to one's friend. One implants confidence in one's friend to have a go, perhaps for the first time. To encourage means to 'put courage in'. The friend receives a new and fuller awareness of his own powers, strength and self-sufficiency. Encouragement says, 'Have a go, you can do it.'[11]

It is strange that many parents and teachers think that criticism will make a child work harder. In fact it usually destroys what little confidence and incentive the child may have already developed. On the other hand a child that has felt appreciated and has received enough encouragement can even hear some positive criticism. No one finds correction easy, but when it is given by a person who is also genuinely encouraging it can be almost palatable.

Appreciation

Frequently people attempting to form a friendship overlook the need to express their appreciation. To fail to put feelings into words is to assume that your friend knows automatically how much he or she is valued. It reminds me of the story my husband likes to tell of a woman in a divorce court who was complaining that her husband never told her that he loved her. The judge turned to the husband to ask if that was correct. 'Yes, Your Honour! I told her when we were first married that I loved her,' the husband answered. 'And I said that if anything ever changed I'd let her know and nothing has.'

A most moving story is told about two priests who had been friends for many years. The friendship was terminated

very tragically when one of the priests was hit by a car and
killed instantly. On being informed of his friend's death
the other priest rushed to the scene of the accident. He
knelt by the side of the dead man, cradled his head in his
arms and sobbing said, 'Don't die! You can't die! I never
told you that I loved you.'[12]

Life is short and friendship is precious yet many will
identify with that surviving priest. We may never have
expressed appreciation for our friends' loyalty, love and
sacrifices over the years. We may never have told them
how much we love them. Maybe our English culture inhibits
such expressions of affection and we may need to find ways
of doing it that are more suited to our temperament. The
English are supposed to be ingenious and inventive and if
we gave it some thought we may be surprised at the sorts
of things we could come up with. A few weeks ago at
one of our retreats I was amazed and encouraged to see
a mixed group of people finding different ways of expressing appreciation. We had been meditating on loving one's
neighbour and then we were asked to make something,
draw something or write something for a 'neighbour' as
an expression of love and appreciation. One man produced
a beautiful collage of dried leaves for an elderly lady he
visits. Several people wrote a piece of prose for a spouse or
a friend. Yet others drew pictures or made amusing cards.
We all found ways of saying something appreciative without
really violating our English reserve.

Shared Activities

Boredom is one of the enemies of any relationship and
good friends need to build in a variety of shared activities
to keep the friendship alive and fresh. Sharing fun can
revitalise a relationship which has become rather stagnant.
A short while ago I attended a 'creative weekend' with a
friend. We did it for fun and relaxation. It turned out to
be an hilarious experience. Using our imaginations and
a variety of different materials we were given the task
of building an island the size of a dining-room table. It

had to be built to scale and populated. It would have been easy except that we had to work at our bit in total silence in conjunction with eight other people. We laughed about it for weeks afterwards.

Shared activities can also strengthen and cement a friendship. With this same friend I attended a course in Hawaii. Besides the shared learning experience we enjoyed the excitement of snorkelling and swimming together amongst some of the world's most exotic and colourful fish. The memory of such an amazing experience will last for the rest of our lives.

David always laughs when he remembers how his sister-in-law told him she and his older brother read poetry together during their courtship days. Apparently neither of them really liked poetry, they discovered later, but they liked sharing together.

Even work can become fun when shared. I first became friends with my husband, David, when he was still an assistant curate at St Ebbe's Church in Oxford. We painted a part of the church hall interior together. C. S. Lewis writes that companionship, which friendship supervenes, is built on shared activities. Out of these shared activities friendship will sometimes emerge. He goes on to say that, 'Friendship must be about something even if it were only an enthusiasm for dominoes or white mice. Those who have nothing can share nothing; those who are going nowhere can have no fellow-travellers.'[13]

Worship

A shared activity which should keep the friendship healthy is worship and prayer. When two people, whose faith in Jesus is the most important factor in their lives, become friends this shared faith is bound to need expression. In fact this expression is frequently the crowning moment of friendship. Many times when we have been with friends on a speaking tour or on holiday far away from home, we have ended a happy, active day by breaking bread together. Shared spiritual experiences enrich a friendship.

For Consideration:
How much of your friend's past history do you know?
Ask your friend how encouraging he or she finds you to
be?
How did you feel when you read the story of the two
priests?
Could you find a way to show your friend how much
you appreciate him or her in the next few days?
Is there any real fun in your friendships?
Can you remember the last time you spent time worshipping
God with your friend?

Trust

Too many children have grown up in an environment of
inconsistency and unreliability where mistrust comes more
naturally than trust, but trust is the indispensable factor in
a friendship. Without it fear and suspicion will haunt the
relationship and it will never really develop into a whole-
some friendship. Once trust has been established care must
be taken to maintain it and ensure that nothing happens to
hurt it. There are several things which can severely damage
trust.

Unreliability

'Trust requires that I can predict the other person's re-
sponses or behaviour with some accuracy; I can depend
on him or her abiding by certain consistencies. If I cannot,
then trust is very tentative.'[14]

When a friend forgets a commitment, breaks a promise
or is late for an outing, trust is automatically undermined.
Even though forgiveness is given and received many times,
if this becomes the norm in the relationship the foundation
for a close friendship may be slowly eroded and eventually be snuffed out altogether.

Insincerity

The word 'sincere' in Latin means 'without wax'. In Roman
times 'sometimes vendors would sell their marble with its

flaws filled in with wax and thus deceive the purchaser. Marble without wax was genuine through and through. It was honestly what it appeared to be . . . sincere.'[15]

A sincere friend can be trusted to mean what he says and to do what he promises. Some people find it difficult to disagree or to use the little word 'no'. They feel it negates friendship. Actually agreeing to something which would be impossible, take too long, or be inappropriate is more damaging to friendship in the long run. Saint Paul writes of 'speaking the truth in love'.[16] Truth mixed with love are vital ingredients in real friendship.

Occasionally a person may fall into the trap of dishonesty with a close friend sincerely thinking it is for the best. For example in a desire to protect a friend you may avoid telling him about some future happening you fear will cause him pain. You may pretend that all is well, or even tell an outright lie in your effort to spare your friend distress. In this way you not only treat him as if he were a child, but you also deny him the opportunity to work through the problem. Eventually when the truth comes to light, one's friend has to face not only the painful facts but also your dishonesty and belittling treatment. We can never protect one another from pain and problems – they are part of living. However, we can help one another to face the truth and lovingly support one another as we work through the pain that the truth may bring.

Moodiness
One of the comforting aspects of friendship is getting to know another person well and being able to depend on the known character of one's friend. Fluctuating moods can be very damaging to trust. Babies learn to trust by experiencing reliable, even monotonous mothering. It is detrimental to trust when one can never depend upon the mood of one's friend. One day he or she may be happy and chatty, then for no apparent reason she withdraws into silence. No one is totally free of moodiness but

to be changeable with no explanation puts extraordinary strain on any close relationship.

For Consideration:
Take a risk and ask your friend how reliable, honest and dependable he or she finds you to be. It must be a frank reply. Of the four basic requirements, commitment is the most difficult to develop to the satisfaction of both parties. In the next chapter we will examine the type of commitment needed to build a lasting friendship.

11

COMMITMENT TO FRIENDSHIP

Anne has many friends with whom she likes to keep in touch. The problem is time. She reminds me of the circus plate spinner who rushes up and down a long line trying to keep all the plates in motion at once. Anne only has enough time to drop a postcard or ring her friends once in a while just to remind them that she is thinking of them. There is not enough time for any one of these relationships to become special. In fact they would be better described as incidental or casual friendships which are undemanding and have a limited commitment – only in terms of keeping in touch. Some people prefer these less committed relationships and therefore choose to have many casual acquaintances rather than a few special friends, who would inevitably demand a much higher level of commitment.

True friendship is a relationship which has moved through the preliminary stages of issuing formal invitations and getting acquainted but has not stopped there, as many do. It has progressed to a point where both know that with each other they feel 'at home'. Broadcaster Margaret Jay exemplified this when she described her relationship with her best friend and said, 'We're not visitors in each other's lives.'[1]

As time passes a commitment to the relationship develops until a strong, healthy friendship exists which should be of immense benefit to both. The early days of a relationship are the time for open discussion about the expectations and hopes for its future. The moment we commit to something or someone we forgo a certain degree of freedom. Balancing

freedom against commitment is a hard job in friendship
and many a relationship comes unstuck at this point. Two
friends told me of the difficulty they had resolving the problem of their differing levels of commitment. One felt she
needed some commitment with regard to the future and the
other felt she needed to be totally free to move on whenever
she felt so inclined. Only by prayer and discussion did they
come to an understanding and an eventual agreement.

Commitment only militates against freedom when under-
taken legalistically. Friendship has no need of any formal,
legally binding contract, unless, of course, there has been
some sort of financial agreement, as in buying a home
together. In reality the only commitment which exists between friends is the commitment to love one another. Of
course love carries with it certain obligations and some
structure may be needed to give the friendship cohesion.
The outworking of the following obligations may differ in
each friendship. Nevertheless I would see them as basic to
a committed relationship.

A Commitment to the Well-being of one's Friend

We all have a tendency to be more 'ego-centred' than
'others-centred'. Our own needs cry out to be met and
it is not easy to forgo immediate satisfaction in order first
to meet the needs of another. But love requires that one
lays aside one's own needs in order to seek the well-being
of one's friend.

'In theory, love implies a basic attitude of concern for
the satisfaction, security and development of the one loved.
In practice, love implies that I am ready and willing to
forgo my own convenience, to invest my own time, and
even to risk my own security to promote your satisfaction,
security and development.'[2] This is the theory! When we
commit to friendship this is what is implied in that commitment. However, many who thrill at the excitement, joy
and satisfaction of having a close friend never realise that
sacrifice is part of the package.

A Commitment to Openness

In the beginning of a relationship the sharing of thoughts, opinions, values and some feelings is exciting and rewarding. It is part of the process of getting to know one another. Honest communication becomes more difficult when the friendship has run on for some time and the differences begin to put a little strain on the relationship; hopes have not been met in the absolute way expected; minor irritations have become magnified and the friendship no longer seems such a good idea after all. The only way forward at this point is to be honest and open about what is happening. John Powell calls this 'an emotional clearance'.[3]

Janet and Erica had been friends for about a year. The friendship had started well. They appeared to have a lot in common and were pursuing the same goals of growth and wholeness in Christ. They met frequently to pray together and help one another towards their objective. Then the glamour of the early months began to wear off and they became rather cool and distant towards each other. I watched the relationship deteriorate and longed to sit them down to talk honestly and openly about their feelings. In fact circumstances eventually forced them to face up to the breakdown of their relationship and as a result they spent several hours talking through all the problems. As they aired their differences God brought them to a place of understanding and reconciliation. When I last saw them there was a marked difference in their attitude to one another. Gone was the hard tone of voice and the guarded look in the eye. Instead their voices and eyes held only affection and kindness towards one another.

Only through open discussion can a friendship evolve to a place of healthy reality. It takes courage and determination to stay with the pain of speaking and hearing truth until that 'emotional clearance' has taken place. Out of the discomfort an authentic and solid friendship will emerge.

'Speaking the truth in love' is not easy but the end result should be growth. 'Speaking the truth in love, we will in all things grow up into him who is the Head, that is, Christ.'[4]

There are two main points to remember when one is trying to be honest and open with one's friend. The first is 'when' and the second is 'how'. Unless you know that you have a problem with procrastination it is a good policy to wait and pray before you speak out about something which could be hurtful to your friend. Many times I have wanted to tackle an issue with a friend before it turned into a big problem and yet the very act of mentioning it would have made it sound bigger than it really was. So I have waited, praying for the right moment to say it and the right way to put it across. Often as I have bided my time my friend has brought the subject up, asking for my opinion and I have been able to come in with both the positive and negative aspects in an unthreatening manner. Usually in a long-term relationship there is no urgent need to get things sorted out immediately, unless there is a real threat to communication. A problem can be shelved until the right time and the best way of approaching it has been found. Only when the difficulty is causing strong emotions, upsetting the harmony and blocking rapport should one be in a hurry to resolve it.

A Commitment to Loyalty

Every friendship has some minimal obligations and early in the relationship these should be discussed. Once understood and agreed to they then become an accepted part of the relationship. When something arises to challenge or change things this should be openly talked about. Loyalty breaks down when these obligations are not met. When I was at boarding school the obligations pertaining to best friends were quite simple. We partnered each other on our weekend walks, chose one another for team games and invited each other to our birthday parties. These were understood by everyone and it would have been considered a breach of loyalty to have failed in these minimal obligations.

As I have already mentioned Prue Bedwell and I, as well as being friends, work together. This means we often need to sit down with our diaries and allow each other access to our future plans. We decide on the meetings we should do together and discuss the ones we should do on our own. It would be disloyal for one of us to accept an engagement without first approaching the other for an opinion and comment, and the first option to be part of it. This access to each other's diaries applies very much to our work relationship, but similarly it applies to our friendship. Friendship is not something one uses when one feels like it, or something one switches on and off at one's convenience. Friends are a part of one's life. Therefore it is important to involve one another in future planning. This is not necessarily for the purpose of doing everything together, but in order to allow the other access to one's life and to allow plenty of time for the relationship.

Loyalty also means standing by one's friend during the difficult times. I was talking to a woman who has a very demanding job. Her best friend was sick and she felt committed to supporting and being available to her friend until she was well. Friendship demands this type of loyalty. It requires us to 'rejoice with those who rejoice and mourn with those who mourn'.[5] A friend may even have a long-term problem and one could easily feel bored hearing the same story day after day. Or perhaps a friend is grieving and the process seems to go on for ever. Friendship necessitates one standing firm and giving the needed support because 'a friend loves at all times'.[6]

Loyalty involves standing up for one's friends when they are criticised. It also means never discrediting them to others. Lastly, loyalty demands that secrets shared by one's friends are never divulged. Probably the greatest disloyalty and injury to trust is the breaking of such confidences.

A Commitment to Perseverance

John Powell sees communication as being the life-blood of love and the guarantee of its growth. He also sees it as the essence of love in practice.[7] Certainly many friendships fall short at this point, and many would identify with the distraught priest who had never told his friend how much he loved him, until it was too late. A college girl once wrote in her journal that if she had only a short time to live she would contact all the people she had ever really loved and make sure they knew she had loved them.[8]

This type of communication is the normal work of love. However, one must be careful not to mistake discussion for communication. It is easy to fall into the trap of discussing the pros and cons of a loving relationship and never getting around to either truly communicating one's love, or of actually putting love into practice. 'We would rather debate, think about and question these realities than put them into practice.'[9] I can think about and discuss my belief that love means making time for the one I love, but unless I actually make that space, the work of love never gets done.

During a practical discussion on love a group of people were asked to write down the words: 'Love is . . .' Then they were asked to fill the gap with their ideas. Some interesting suggestions were written down and then read out to the group:

'Love is sharing a meal'
'Love is spending time together'
'Love is listening'
'Love is giving a compliment'
'Love is making a cup of tea'
'Love is getting up first in the morning'
'Love is making a cake'
'Love is making a phone-call'

If communication is the life-blood of a friendship then we must not only work at it when it is easy but also when it is hard. We must persevere until we have conquered our personal hang-ups, fears and embarrassments. At the same time we must work at maintaining the relationship and saying 'I love you' in other ways. Finding creative ways of keeping a relationship alive is very difficult for some people. Some lack initiative and ideas, and others are just too lazy to make the effort. But none of us should expect to enjoy the benefits of friendship without playing our part in perseverance and hard work.

A Commitment to Giving Time

The sort of relationship we have been describing requires time – time for it to develop and grow. Not everyone is temperamentally suited to such an intimate relationship and would prefer to have many casual friendships rather than one or two close ones. It is true that we cannot have a deep, sharing relationship with many people. There is not enough time, nor do we have the capacity to interact in a deeply personal and loving way with many people.[10] Henry Adams was pretty near the truth when he said, 'One friend in a lifetime is much, two are many, three are hardly possible.'

Perhaps the amount of time available should be thought about before a friendship is pursued in a serious way because automatically with the decision to be friends comes a commitment of time. This commitment is difficult for some people to make. They may already have too many other people making a demand upon them. In this case a friendship of a more casual nature may be preferable. It is important that this is made clear from the outset of the relationship.

The two friends who shared with me the problems they were experiencing with regard to their expectations of friendship had quite different ideas about the commitment of time. One enjoyed many casual friendships and had an erratic, demanding job. When asked what were her expectations of this relationship she replied, 'Friendship, fun and fellowship.' These were great hopes but rather unrealistic. She had to face the fact that such expectations would demand a higher degree of commitment than she had previously anticipated. Her new friend on the other hand was less outgoing, had a more predictable job and was ready to make a significant commitment to the relationship. Once this difference in attitude was recognised they both decided they must go away and think more seriously about the sort of relationship they wanted to pursue.

Any discussion on commitment should include the length of the commitment. Should one make a commitment to be friends for a short time, a long time or for a lifetime? In other words is the relationship a permanent one? John Powell certainly feels that a commitment of love, at whatever level, has to be a permanent one. If you say that you are a friend, you will always be a friend, not as long as or until anything. You will always be there for your friend. Any other kind of love, he feels, loses its effect. We need to know that the love on offer is permanent before we give up our security operations, our masks, our roles and our games. We cannot commit to a temporary, tentative love, to an offer which has all that fine print and many footnotes in the contract.[11]

I would agree that love can never be conditional. However, we have to accept that life situations change. At this present time I have several close friends. I believe I will love them always, but I may not be close to them always. Some of my best friends are now living thousands of miles away in South America. I hold them in great affection and that will never change. Whenever there is a chance to be together I will devote as much time to be with them as I possibly can, but it is unlikely that we can ever pursue the friendship in the same way as we formerly did. Therefore I would suggest that the commitment to love should be permanent, but the commitment to enjoy a close, sharing relationship may not be.

For Consideration:
Are you the sort of person who could commit to this type of relationship?
Do you function better in casual friendships?
Are you giving anyone false hopes with respect to your commitment to them?
If you have a close friendship are you prepared to commit in the ways discussed?

If you are, which of the above obligations do you find most difficult and will need to be worked on?

Freedom

Individual freedom is essential to growth and wholeness and a firm commitment to friendship should not militate against this. In fact a friendship which has stood the test of time should give one a sense of freedom. One can relax in a relationship where one is free from the worry that one's friend is going to let one down either through disloyalty, unreliability or dishonesty. Even mistakes and let-downs, which are bound to occur in any human relationship, can be overlooked at this point because an underlying trust has been firmly established.

Freedom should be the healthy outcome of love, sharing, trust and commitment. Predictability, in the sense of being familiar with the habits of one's friend, frees one to be able to enjoy the relationship without the anxiety of not knowing what to expect next. Commitment frees one from clinging on too tightly for fear of losing one's friend. At this point it is possible to appreciate and enjoy one's separateness and differences. It is essential that a friendship grows towards freedom, not loss of it. Only trust and commitment will enable it to do so.

Space

Personal freedom is important to maintain in any relationship. So also is space. It is vital for one's health and growth that one maintains a certain degree of emotional and physical space. With both strangers and acquaintances personal boundaries are placed at a comfortable distance. Usually these are politely respected. Conversation is kept at a safe level and physical distance is maintained. As friendship develops the two people involved unconsciously negotiate their space until they have reached a mutually acceptable and more intimate position. However, lack of commitment and mistrust could cause a person to move in too close. Unconsciously one may feel that continual contact will somehow prevent the feared loss. On the other hand mistrust could result in too great a distance being retained. When this happens the friendship never really prospers.

The amount of personal space each one requires for comfort is influenced by one's culture and personal history. On arrival in South America we soon discovered the Chileans' need for privacy was far less than our own. After nearly seventeen years we still sometimes found their extremely personal questions hard to handle. Even my husband David found it difficult. Born into a large family, with a brother only eleven months younger than himself, he is gregarious and seems not to need too much space around him. Whereas I was born the last in a family with two sisters and a brother much older than myself. I was accustomed to having time and privacy to think my thoughts and to feel my feelings without interruption. Now I need time to be alone and feel distinctly uncomfortable if my emotional space is invaded except by those I know very well.

In a healthy friendship where love, sharing, trust and commitment are growing, personal needs for space should be respected. Certainly Jesus required time away from his disciples and 'often withdrew to lonely places and prayed'.[12] For a relationship to be truly enriching there has to be space. 'All too often we fail to allow each other enough solitude – solitude of heart as well as physical solitude. Our fear tells us that togetherness is based on physical presence to each other, and complete openness. Whereas it is the safeguarding of physical and emotional space that will lead to genuine closeness. Moreover, everyone, within marriage or friendship, needs an inner enclosure, the door of which is open only to God. For deep intimacy in relationship requires an area of inviolable privacy.'[13]

In the end the secret of friendship lies in maintaining this inner enclosure with an open door to God. Jesus is our greatest friend and He alone can teach us how to love one another. Jesus is the light of the world and our transparency and honesty with ourselves and with others depends totally on our closeness with Him.

Prayer
Heavenly Father, I thank you for your Son, Jesus. I thank you that he showed us what true love was like. I ask you to help me to be a good friend to ... Help me to love ... Help us share our lives with each other. Help us to grow in trust one for the other and show me when I fail to be trustworthy. Help me to make an appropriate commitment to this friendship, but help me also to allow the proper freedom and space for my friend to grow and develop as an individual. Most of all, I ask you to help me to keep the inner sanctum only for you, where I may meet with you and grow in loving you, trusting you and in commitment to you. May this friendship and my life bring glory to Jesus, in whose name I ask this. Amen.

NOTES

Introduction
1 Gen. 2:18
2 Bourne, F. W., *Billy Bray, The King's Son* (Epworth Press 1937), p.62.
3 Powell, John, *Unconditional Love* (Argus Communications 1978, Tx 75002), p.92.
4 Matt. 22:37,39
5 Pytches, Mary, *A Child No More* (Hodder & Stoughton 1991), p.24.

Chapter 1. A Description of Friendship
1 Exley, Helen, *To A Very Special Friend*, selected by Helen Exley. Exley Pub. Ltd, Watford 1991.
2 Powell, John, *The Secret of Staying in Love* (Tabor Publishing, Texas 1974), p.44.
3 1 Cor. 13:4
4 1 Cor. 12:31
5 Rom. 13:8
6 Marshall, Tom, *Understanding Leadership* (Sovereign World, Chichester 1991), p.141.
7 Source unknown.
8 Source unknown.
9 Exley, *To A Very Special Friend*.
10 Marshall, Tom, *Right Relationships* (Sovereign World, England 1989), p.33.
11 Powell, John, & Brady, Loretta, *Will The Real Me Please Stand Up* (Tabor Publishing, Texas).
12 Exley, *To A Very Special Friend*.

Chapter 2. Whose Idea Anyway?

1 Gen. 1:26
2 Marshall, Tom, *Right Relationships* (Sovereign World, Chichester 1989), p.16.
3 Gen. 2:18
4 Prov. 18:24
5 Isa. 41:8; Jas. 2:23
6 Exod. 33:11
7 Num. 12:6,7,8
8 Marshall, *Right Relationships*, p.29.
9 1 Sam. 18:1–4
10 1 Sam. 20:41,42
11 2 Sam. 1:25,26
12 Lewis, C. S., *The Four Loves* (Collins, London 1960), p.55.
13 Ruth 1:16–18
14 John 15:9,12–15
15 John 19:26,27
16 Col. 4:14
17 2 Tim. 4:11
18 Ecc. 4:9

Chapter 3. The Blessings of Friendship

1 Cotton, Charles Caleb (1780–1832), Peter, Laurence J., *Quotations for Our Time* (Souvenir Press, London 1977), p.214.
2 Prov. 18:1
3 Lewis, C. S., *The Four Loves* (Collins, London 1960), p.7.
4 Prov. 27:6
5 White, John, *Eros Defiled* (Inter-Varsity Press, Leicester 1977), p.77.
6 Scott Peck, M., *The Road Less Travelled* (Simon and Schuster, New York 1978), p.153.
7 Prov. 27:17
8 Prov. 27:9
9 Powell, John, *Unconditional Love* (Argus Communications, Texas 1978), p.88.

10 Eccles. 4:10–12
11 Powell, *Unconditional Love*, p.94.
12 John. 3:29
13 Eccles. 4:8,9
14 Marshall, Tom, *Right Relationships* (Sovereign World, Chichester 1989), p.58.
15 2 John: 12
16 Eccles. 4:12
17 Rev. 21:3,4
18 Exley, Helen, *To A Very Special Friend*, selected by Helen Exley. Exley Pub. Ltd, Watford 1991.
19 Powell, John, *The Secret of Staying in Love* (Tabor Pub., California 1974), p.67.

Chapter 4. Hindrances to Making Friends

1 Ps. 133
2 Subby, Robert, *Lost in the Shuffle* (Health Communications Inc., Florida 1987), p.67.
3 Comiskey, Andy, *Pursuing Sexual Wholeness* (Desert Stream Ministries, California 1988), p.48.
4 Erikson, Erik, *Childhood and Society* (Collins, London 1977).
5 Lewis, C. S., *The Four Loves* (Collins Press, London 1960), p.8.
6 Lake, Frank, *Clinical Theology* (abridged by Martin H. Yeomans) (Darton, Longman and Todd, London 1986), p.21.

Chapter 5. Obstacles to Maintaining a Healthy Friendship

1 Beattie, Melody, *Codependent No More* (Harper and Row, San Francisco 1987), p.70.
2 ibid., p.78.
3 Lake, Frank, *Tight Corners in Pastoral Counselling* (Darton, Longman and Todd, London 1981), p.19.
4 Lake, Frank, *Clinical Theology* (abridged by Martin H. Yeomans) (Darton, Longman and Todd, London 1986), p.90.

Chapter 6. The Trap of Emotional Dependency
1 Ps. 41:7,9
2 Ps. 55:12,14
3 Prov. 12:26
4 Jer. 17:9
5 Comiskey, Andy, *Pursuing Sexual Wholeness* (Desert Stream Ministries, California 1988), p.208.
6 Powell, John, *The Secret of Staying in Love* (Tabor Pub., Texas 1974), p.103.
7 Ps. 139:23
8 Ps. 139:13
9 Powell, John, *Unconditional Love* (Argus Communications, Texas 1978), p.86.
10 Wallace, Marjorie, 'One in a hundred' (*Telegraph Magazine*, December 7, 1991), p.38.
11 Payne, Leanne, *Crisis in Masculinity* (Kingsway Publications, Eastbourne 1985), p.96.
12 ibid., p.26.
13 Jer. 17:5
14 Jer. 2:11
15 Jer. 2:13
16 Comiskey, *Pursuing Sexual Wholeness*, p.60.
17 Jer. 2:25
18 Jas. 5:16

Chapter 7. The Trap of Co-dependency
1 Hemfelt, R., Minirth, F., Meier, P., *Love is a Choice* (Monarch Pub. 1990), p.11.
2 Beattie, Melody, *Codependent No More* (Harper and Row, New York 1987), p.31.
3 Luke 5:42,43
4 John 5:30
5 Hemfelt et al., *Love is a Choice*, p.65.
6 Lewis, C. S., *The Four Loves* (Collins, London 1960), p.43.
7 ibid., p.36.

Chapter 8. Out of Bounds
1 Gen. 3:6
2 Llewellyn, Richard, *How Green Was My Valley* (Michael Joseph, London 1939), p.368.
3 Thorkelson-Rentzel, Lori, *Emotional Dependency* (Exodus International North America 1987), p.1.
4 White, John, *Eros Defiled* (Inter-Varsity Press, England 1977), p.82.
5 Matt. 10:16
6 Jude 21 (Living Bible).
7 Rom. 12:17
8 Jer. 17:9
9 Powell, John, *The Secret of Staying in Love* (Tabor Pub., Texas 1974), p.60.
10 Luke 15:17
11 Jas. 5:16

Chapter 9. Healing the Wounded Child
1 Jer. 17:10
2 Ps. 139:23,24
3 John 8:32
4 Pytches, Mary, *A Healing Fellowship* (Hodder & Stoughton, London 1988), p.134.
5 Llewellyn, Richard, *How Green Was My Valley* (Michael Joseph, London 1939), p.15.
6 Comiskey, Andy, *Pursuing Sexual Wholeness* (Creation House, Florida 1988), p.181.
7 Isa. 61:1
8 Dan. 2:22
9 Job. 33:14–15
10 Hemfelt, R., Minirth, F., Meier, P., *Love is a Choice* (Monarch Pub. 1990), p.232.
11 Matt. 18:35
12 Matt. 5:4
13 Isa. 61:1
14 2 Cor. 5:17

Chapter 10. The Work of Friendship
1 Powell, John, *The Secret of Staying in Love* (Tabor Pub., California 1974), p.69.
2 1 Cor. 13
3 1 Cor. 13:5
4 Powell, *The Secret of Staying in Love*, p.147.
5 *Reader's Digest,* December 1991 *(Los Angeles Times Syndicate).*
6 McDowell, Josh, *The Secret of Loving* (Here's Life Pub. 1985), p.93.
7 *Chambers Everyday Dictionary*, (W & R Chambers Ltd, Edinburgh 1975).
8 McDowell, *The Secret of Loving*, p.101,
9 Col. 3:12–14
10 McDowell, *The Secret of Loving*, p.45.
11 Powell, John, *Unconditional Love* (Argus Communications 1978, Tx. 75002), p.86.
12 Powell, *The Secret of Staying in Love*, p.122.
13 Lewis, C. S., *The Four Loves* (Collins, London 1960), p.63.
14 Marshall, Tom, *Right Relationships* (Sovereign World, Chichester 1989), p.73.
15 Pytches, Mary, *Set My People Free* (Hodder & Stoughton, London 1987), p.96.
16 Eph. 4:15

Chapter 11. Commitment to Friendship
1 Billington, Joy, 'Best friends' (*Women's Journal*, December 1989).
2 Powell, John, *The Secret of Staying in Love* (Tabor Pub., California 1974), p.44.
3 ibid., p.73.
4 Eph. 4:15
5 Rom. 12:15
6 Prov. 17:17
7 Powell, *The Secret of Staying in Love*, p.70.
8 ibid., p.150.
9 ibid., p.71.

10 ibid., p.47.
11 ibid., p.53.
12 Luke 5:16
13 Magdalen, Margaret, CSMV, *Transformed By Love* (Darton, Longman and Todd, London 1989), p.75.

Hodder Christian Paperbacks: a tradition of excellence.

Great names and great books to enrich your life and meet
your needs. Choose from such authors as:

Corrie ten Boom	Jackie Pullinger
Charles Colson	David Pytches
Richard Foster	Mary Pytches
Billy Graham	Jennifer Rees Larcombe
Michael Green	Cliff Richard
Michele Guinness	John Stott
Joyce Huggett	Joni Eareckson Tada
Francis MacNutt	Colin Urquhart
Catherine Marshall	David Watson
Jim Packer	David Wilkerson
Adrian Plass	John Wimber

The wide range of books on the Hodder Christian Paper-
back list include biography, personal testimony, devotional
books, evangelistic books, Christian teaching, fiction, drama,
poetry, books that give help for times of need – and many
others.

Ask at your nearest Christian bookshop or at your church
bookstall for the latest titles.

SOME BESTSELLERS IN HODDER CHRISTIAN PAPERBACKS

THE HIDING PLACE by Corrie ten Boom

The triumphant story of Corrie ten Boom, heroine of the anti-Nazi underground.

"A brave and heartening story."

Baptist Times

GOD'S SMUGGLER by Brother Andrew

An international bestseller. God's Smuggler carries contraband Bibles past armed border guards to bring the love of Christ to the people behind the Iron Curtain.

"A book you will not want to miss."

Catherine Marshall

DISCIPLESHIP by David Watson

". . . breath-taking, block-busting, Bible-based simplicity on every page."

Jim Packer

LISTENING TO GOD by Joyce Huggett

A profound spiritual testimony, and practical help for discovering a new dimension of prayer.

"This is counselling at its best."

Leadership Today